I0026904

Princess Diana

Modern Day Moon-Goddess

Books by Jane G. Goldberg, Ph.D.

The Psychotherapeutic Treatment of Cancer Patients
The Dark Side of Love: The Positive Role of Negative Feelings
Deceits of the Mind (and Their Effects on the Body)
InSPArations: If You Can Do It at a Spa, You Can Do it at Home
Princess Diana, Modern Day Moon-Goddess: A Psychoanalytical and Mythological
      Look at Diana Spencer's Life, Marriage, and Death (with Lochlainn Seabrook)
The Hormesis Effect: The Miraculous Healing Power of Radioactive Stones (with Jay
      Gutierrez)
My Mother, My Daughter, My Self

Books by Colonel Lochlainn Seabrook

ADULTS (partial list)
Britannia Rules: Goddess-Worship in Ancient Anglo-Celtic Society - An Academic Look
      at the United Kingdom's Matricentric Spiritual Past
Seabrook's Bible Dictionary of Traditional and Mystical Christian Doctrines
Jesus and the Law of Attraction: The Bible-Based Guide to Creating Perfect Health,
      Wealth, and Happiness Following Christ's Simple Formula
Christ Is All and In All: Rediscovering Your Divine Nature and the Kingdom Within
The Bible and the Law of Attraction: 99 Teachings of Jesus, the Apostles, and the
      Prophets
Jesus and the Gospel of Q: Christ's Pre-Christian Teachings As Recorded in the New
      Testament
Christmas Before Christianity: How the Birthday of the "Sun" Became the Birthday of
      the "Son"
The Book of Kelle: An Introduction to Goddess-Worship and the Great Celtic Mother-
      Goddess Kelle, Original Blessed Lady of Ireland
The Goddess Dictionary of Words and Phrases: Introducing a New Core Vocabulary
      for the Women's Spirituality Movement
Aphrodite's Trade: The Hidden History of Prostitution Unveiled
UFOs and Aliens: The Complete Guidebook
Everything You Were Taught About the Civil War is Wrong, Ask a Southerner!
Everything You Were Taught About American Slavery is Wrong, Ask a Southerner!
All We Ask is to be Let Alone: The Southern Secession Fact Book
Abraham Lincoln Was a Liberal, Jefferson Davis Was a Conservative: The Missing Key
      to Understanding the American Civil War
The Great Yankee Coverup: What the North Doesn't Want You to Know About
      Lincoln's War
Confederate Flag Facts: What Every American Should Know About Dixie's Southern
      Cross

CHILDREN
Honest Jeff and Dishonest Abe: A Southern Children's Guide to the Civil War
Saddle, Sword, and Gun: A Biography of Nathan Bedford Forrest For Teens

Princess Diana

Modern Day Moon-Goddess

A PSYCHOANALYTICAL & MYTHOLOGICAL LOOK
AT DIANA SPENCER'S LIFE, MARRIAGE, & DEATH

Jane G. Goldberg, Ph.D.
Colonel Lochlainn Seabrook

FOREWORD BY PHYLLIS W. MEADOW. PH.D.

2017
SEA RAVEN PRESS, NASHVILLE, TENNESSEE, USA

PRINCESS DIANA, MODERN DAY MOON-GODDESS

Published by
Sea Raven Press, Cassidy Ravensdale, President
PO Box 1484, Spring Hill, Tennessee 37174-1484 USA
www.searavenpress.com • searavenpress@gmail.com

1ˢᵗ SRP paperback edition, 1ˢᵗ printing: June 1997, ISBN: 978-0-9821899-0-0
1ˢᵗ SRP paperback edition, 2ⁿᵈ printing: October 2008, ISBN: 978-0-9821899-0-0
1ˢᵗ SRP paperback edition, 3ʳᵈ printing, revised: May 2014, ISBN: 978-0-9821899-0-0
1ˢᵗ SRP paperback edition, 4ᵗʰ printing: July 2017, ISBN: 978-0-9821899-0-0
1ˢᵗ SRP hardcover edition, 1ˢᵗ printing: July 2017, ISBN: 978-1-943737-53-6

Copyright © 1997, 2008, 2014, 2017 Sea Raven Press
in accordance with U.S. and international copyright laws and regulations, as stated and protected under the Berne Union for the Protection of Literary and Artistic Property (Berne Convention), and the Universal Copyright Convention (the UCC). All rights reserved under the Pan-American and International Copyright Conventions.

ISBN: 978-0-9821899-0-0 (paperback)
Library of Congress Control Number: 2014940538

This work is the copyrighted intellectual property of Sea Raven Press and has been registered with the Copyright Office at the Library of Congress in Washington, D.C., USA. No part of this work (including text, covers, drawings, photos, illustrations, maps, images, diagrams, etc.), in whole or in part, may be used, reproduced, stored in a retrieval system, or transmitted, in any form or by any means now known or hereafter invented, without written permission from the publisher. The sale, duplication, hire, lending, copying, digitalization, or reproduction of this material, in any manner or form whatsoever, is also prohibited, and is a violation of federal, civil, and digital copyright law, which provides severe civil and criminal penalties for any violations.

Princess Diana, Modern Day Moon-Goddess: A Psychoanalytical and Mythological Look at Diana Spencer's Life, Marriage, and Death, by Dr. Jane G. Goldberg and Lochlainn Seabrook. Foreword by Dr. Phyllis W. Meadow. Includes an index and bibliographical references.

Front and back cover design and art, book design, layout, and interior art by Lochlainn Seabrook
All images, graphic design, graphic art, and illustrations copyright © Lochlainn Seabrook
Cover images & design copyright © Lochlainn Seabrook
Cover image: "Princess Diana," circa 1998, from a postage stamp

The paper used in this book is acid-free and lignin-free. It has been certified by the Sustainable Forestry Initiative and the Forest Stewardship Council and meets all ANSI standards for archival quality paper.

PRINTED & MANUFACTURED IN OCCUPIED TENNESSEE, FORMER CONFEDERATE STATES OF AMERICA

DEDICATION

To Lady Diana Spencer, Princess of Wales. In life and death a universally beloved Moon-Child who wore the lunar crescent crown of her ancient namesake.

EPIGRAPH

"The Eternal Feminine draws us on high."

Goethe

Contents

SEA RAVEN PRESS
—INSPIRING BOOKS—
For the Whole Family
SeaRavenPress.com
NASHVILLE, TENNESSEE

CANTICLE OF BROTHER SUN AND SISTER MOON

Most high, all powerful, all good Lord! All praise is yours, all glory, all honor, and all blessing. To you, alone, Most High, do they belong. No mortal lips are worthy to pronounce your name.

Be praised, my Lord, through all your creatures, especially through my lord Brother Sun, who brings the day; and you give light through him. And he is beautiful and radiant in all his splendor! Of you, Most High, he bears the likeness.

Be praised, my Lord, through Sister Moon and the stars; in the heavens you have made them, precious and beautiful.

Be praised, my Lord, through Brothers Wind and Air, and clouds and storms, and all the weather, through which you give your creatures sustenance.

Be praised, My Lord, through Sister Water; she is very useful, and humble, and precious, and pure.

Be praised, my Lord, through Brother Fire, through whom you brighten the night. He is beautiful and cheerful, and powerful and strong.

Be praised, my Lord, through our sister Mother Earth, who feeds us and rules us, and produces various fruits with colored flowers and herbs.

Be praised, my Lord, through those who forgive for love of you; through those who endure sickness and trial. Happy those who endure in peace, for by you, Most High, they will be crowned.

Be praised, my Lord, through our Sister Bodily Death, from whose embrace no living person can escape. Woe to those who die in mortal sin! Happy those she finds doing your most holy will. The second death can do no harm to them.

Praise and bless my Lord, and give thanks, and serve him with great humility.

☼ St. Francis of Assisi ☾

Italy, 1225

Foreword

"Life is just a journey." — Princess Diana

I am pleased to be asked to write a Foreword to this book; slim though it be, it remains fat with revelations. It discusses specifically the story of Princess Diana, and traces her life and her death through the lens of mythology and psychoanalysis.

The writing is replete with information I did not know. It is a smart, well-researched book, as well as an entertaining book. Though the subject of Diana's seemingly senseless death is a painful one, as the authors see it here, it becomes a death not without meaning, and not without a certain inevitability.

Princess Diana, Modern Day Moon-Goddess achieves the best of what psychoanalysis promises: it gives meaning to phenomena that at first blush appear to be random and due to chance. It is the kind of deep analysis of real-life phenomena, as Goldberg and Seabrook have done here, that is in the tradition of both Jung and Freud, as well as the venerable Robert Graves.

Heartily recommended for an afternoon of tears, intellectual engagement and soul-deep satisfaction.

DR. PHYLLIS W. MEADOW

Prologue

"I'd like to be a queen in people's hearts, but I don't see myself being queen of this country." — Princess Diana

IN THE YEAR 1997 AN event occurred that reverberated around the world. It was startlingly sudden, and collectively—independent of religion, creed or nationality—we came together for a moment in time, sharing our shock and our grief. But even in our mourning, we were confounded by what appeared to be the utter meaninglessness of the death of Diana Spencer—a senseless death that followed a life that had come to hold such profound meaning and further promise. Her death seemed to be such an unfortunate happenstance, such an unlikely convergence of factors—the hunt of the paparazzi, the speed of the car, the alcohol level of the driver, the neglect to fasten seat-belts.

Yet, we hunger for a deeper explanation. We don't want to be satisfied with the explanation of mere bad luck. We seek an explanation that gives a more spiritual understanding to Diana's death, a way of placing her life and her death within some natural and harmonious order of the universe. It is through combining the study of ancient mythology and contemporary psychoanalysis that we can come to this understanding.

In our ancient past there was only one way of ordering experience. This system was the order of the universe; it made the day come after night; it made plants and trees grow and die; it made men and women complete their attraction to one another. It was logical that ancient peoples would choose astronomical and astrological phenomena to order their experience.

Early people lived completely within Nature; each morning their bodies were warmed by the bountiful Sun, and every night their souls were calmed by the cool mist of the Moon. The natural phenomena of the workings of the universe were, in themselves, miraculous, and so it was Nature that became their religion.

The themes of the universe were the themes of their lives: the flux of the seasons, the alternating light of day and night, the growth and death cycles of plants. This was the stuff of their everyday lives, and this was the stuff of their most private, most privileged and most sacred dreams.

In looking at Diana's life and death through the lens of both psychoanalysis and ancient mythology, we can come to a fuller understanding of the forces that pushed and pulled Diana at various angles—forces which led, ultimately, to a high-speed midnight chase on a Parisian street, resulting in her death—a death which, from a mythological perspective, was not an accident at all, but rather, was an entirely predictable event and perhaps the only possible outcome for the life she lived.

Jane G. Goldberg, Ph.D., New York, New York
Colonel Lochlainn Seabrook, Nashville, Tennessee

Princess Diana

Modern Day Moon-Goddess

A PSYCHOANALYTICAL AND MYTHOLOGICAL LOOK
AT DIANA SPENCER'S LIFE, MARRIAGE, AND DEATH

1

The Importance of Myth in Understanding Princess Diana

"I don't go by the rule book. I lead from the heart, not the head." — Princess Diana

W E SUFFER TODAY FROM THE plight of having too few universal stories that we tell to each other. We no longer access collective ways of sharing the experience of being human.

Our early forebears, however, told their stories, and came to understand the commonality of their humanness, through the telling and re-telling of myths. Myths served as their art form, their literature, their historical records, and just as importantly, as the vehicle for the expression of their psychic drives.

Ancient peoples had no articulated concept, as we do today, since the Austrian neurologist and psychiatrist Sigmund Freud, of the unconscious.   Yet, their stories are replete with intuitive understanding of the unconscious. The archetypal themes of birth, natural death, murder, rebirth, rivalry, symbiotic fusion, harmony, and chaos were the raw material of the myths. Myths, in fact, gave order to human drives, impulses, fears, desires, dreams, thoughts, and feelings.

For seventeen years, Diana Spencer, Princess of Wales, gave our contemporary world a story of mythic proportions. It was a story that much of the world shared in creating and enjoying. She became the most famous woman, perhaps the most revered woman, to ever walk the face of the earth.

Upon her death, Earl (Charles Edward) Spencer, in his eulogy to his beloved sister, understood the very human need to make stories; he understood the origin of Diana's fame to have its roots in the kind of story-making that occurred long ago, the stories of myths. The Earl made note of the irony that Diana, whose ancient namesake was that of the mythical goddess of the hunt was, in the end, the most hunted of us all.

If we delve even farther into the mythological and psychological origins of the story that Diana brought to us, comprising her personality, her aspirations, her struggles—indeed, the whole of her life——we come to see that Diana's ultimate fate of an early death had a sense of inevitability to it. Through this dual perspective we can come to see why Diana became a hunted woman, as she was so deftly characterized by her brother.

But additionally, we can see why she became the most popular woman to ever live, why her marriage was doomed to failure, why she eventually came to outshine her husband, and why, finally, she became a victim of the unexpected, horrendous accident that led to her death.

2

Diana & Charles: A Mythic Union

> "There were three of us in this marriage, so it was a bit crowded." — Princess Diana

FROM THE BEGINNING DIANA SPENCER enchanted us. Diana, even before she solemnly took her vows of eternal love and devotion, became one of the most frequently photographed women since the camera was invented.

She was the subject of serious inquiry and interest, and, as well, she was portrayed with warmth in cartoons and comedy. A favorite cartoon was one portraying an obese woman with dark unruly hair showing her hair-dresser a picture of Diana saying, "Make me look like her." Women everywhere aspired to Diana's poise, her elegance and her beauty.

We who remember those heady days of sharing with Diana her successes and her travails were her collective audience. We awaited her every move, felt joy at her pregnancies, and devoured her pictures. Too, we watched her falls and we observed her journey into maturity.

Throughout her reign as a Royal, and even beyond, after her divorce, Diana became an emblem for the women of the world, to be the best that we as women could hope to aspire to and to attain. We identified with her, seeing her as like us. And, too, simultaneously yet in contradistinction, we saw her as different from ourselves, and dreamed of being like her.

The wedding between Diana and Prince Charles Windsor became the most widely observed event of the decade. It was the wedding that all women dreamed of having: a fairy-tale marriage—coming as close to magical realism as this century has known. Theirs was a marital union that seemed to fire the imagination of both the die-hard romantics and the tried and true cynics. It overcame whatever jaded hesitancy we had come to feel about love, true love; we renewed our belief in the possibility of all things good and true.

At first glance, it seems easy enough to understand the collective obsession we had with Diana and her marriage. Charles, as future King, declared his unyielding love for her in his marriage contract. She, Princess, wife, mother, and to-be-Queen, a seemingly down-to-earth, relatively unadorned woman who possessed a kind of dignity, innocence, and decency—an ethereal earthiness. It was just this quality of her being an ordinary, any- kind-of-woman, yet being raised to such extraordinary heights that made the fairy tale such an appealing one.

But the story of Diana and her union to Charles has roots that delve, in fact, much deeper than mere romance. Theirs is a story that touches us at the earliest and most basic level of our identities as man and woman; it is a story whose origins go back to the dawn of our own Anglo-American culture in Greco-Roman times, and finally back to the dawn of humanity itself.

3

Myth & the Gynocentric World

"Anywhere I see suffering, that is where I want to be, doing what I can." — Princess Diana

TO UNDERSTAND THE FULL MEANING of Diana's life, her unhappy marriage to Charles, and her untimely death, we need to go back to an age long ago, even before ancient Greece and Rome. This period, a time span dating from 500,000 years ago to about 10,000 years ago, is known as the Paleolithic.

Extrapolating from archaeological finds in the fossil record from this period, it is clear that our prehistoric ancestors had a profound sense of the unity of all life. There was only one way of ordering experience: by observing the universe itself. Thus, just as the Sun followed the Moon and the Moon followed the Sun, men followed women and women followed men, completing their attraction to one another. There was no separation between the earthly and the spiritual. Spirituality was life and life was spirituality.

Indeed religion as a separate social institution had not yet been created. Why? Because every act, every thought, every event had cosmic significance. The world was simply imbued with religiosity; for there was no distinction between religion and culture, or religion and society.

It was logical that prehistoric peoples would choose astronomical and astrological phenomena to order their everyday lives. They lived within Nature, and each day, it seemed, miracles happened. Every morning their bodies were warmed by the hot golden rays of the self-assured Sun, and every night their souls were calmed by the cool white light of the reticent Moon.

The natural phenomena of the workings of the universe were, in themselves, miraculous enough, and so it was Nature that became their religion. The themes of the universe were the themes of their lives: the flux of the seasons, the alternating light of day and night, the growth and death cycles of vegetation. This was the stuff of human life, and it was the stuff of their most private, most privileged and most sacred dreams. As Thales said, "Everything is full of gods."

Actually "everything was full of goddesses," for during the Paleolithic Age the whole world was entirely Goddess-centered. We know this, in part, because no artistic images of the Male have ever been discovered during this time (in particular during the Lower and Middle Paleolithic); only images of the Female have been found, typically portrayed in clay figurines and cave drawings as large-breasted, faceless, pregnant women, artistic representations known to archaeologists as "Venuses" (after the ancient Roman Goddess of love and sex, Venus).

It is obvious from the existence of prehistoric Venuses—and the utter lack of masculine images—that it was Woman, not Man, who was revered by humanity, and that it was She who embodied the sacred, the power, and the beauty of the Feminine Principle. Indeed, this was a time when every woman was a goddess herself, a time when the Goddess of the Moon ruled and defined everyday life for both women and men around the globe.

Paleolithic human society was, in fact, *gynocentric* (female based) rather than androcentric (male based); *matrilocal* (the husband lived with the wife's family) rather than patrilocal (the wife lives with the husband's family); *matrilineal* (tracing one's descent through the female line) rather than patrilineal (tracing one's descent through the male line); *matrifocal* (concentrated on the principle of motherhood) rather than patrifocal (concentrated on the principle of fatherhood); and *matriarchal* (mother and women were supreme) rather than patriarchal (father and men are supreme).

Why was Woman held in higher esteem than Man during the Paleolithic? It was in great part because paternity, the male's role in reproduction, was not yet known. This simple ignorance of sexual biology prompted our distant ancestors to attribute the Life

Force solely to women, who thus became the human personification of the Female Principle.

Women, it was thought, were self-fertilizing Goddesses, who produced life through the magical procreative power of their own wombs. Additionally, the mysterious correlation between a woman's monthly 28-day menstrual cycle and the lunar 28-day cycle of Earth's nearest celestial neighbor closely identified women with the Moon and with the oceans (due to the sea's lunar-connected tides).

It was Woman's participation in the creation of life alone that was visible and understandable to the ancients. It was Woman who possessed the mysterious milk-bearing breasts, the blood-spilling vulva, and the astonishing life-giving womb. And so it was Woman who became venerated as a goddess, the embodiment of life, love, power, and all that is noble and sacred.

Naturally, from these beliefs the Supreme Being itself was imaged as a female. And so was born the idea of the Great Mother-Goddess, "Creatrix of All Life." The world was not, as is ours, God-centered. It was Goddess-centered. Thus, the first great civilizations were not male-dominant (patriarchal) cultures, but female-dominant (matriarchal) ones; they were cultures that worshiped not "God the Father" but "Goddess the Mother."

In this world, men and women were not seen as equals; rather, women were seen as being superior in all ways. Yet women-ruled peoples and nations were egalitarian and functioned around the idea of cooperation. War between nations was unknown; economies were based on reciprocity, and the cohesive force of the community was this concept of egalitarian cooperation. The body was worshiped and sexual love was considered an act of the most profound spirituality. Sex was religious and religion was sexual. There was no demarcation. To the women and men of this time, following Goddess' commandments of tenderness, generosity and kindness toward others assured them of eternal salvation.

This Goddess-centered world—known today as the Matriarchy or Matriarchate—was not an isolated phenomenon, but one that existed in nearly every culture, worldwide, from the Cro-Magnon people (35,000 B.C.E.) right into the Neolithic period (10,000 B.C.E.). The Goddess Creation Myth was the only one known from Oceania, Asia, and Africa, to the Americas, Europe, and the Middle East. It was Goddess who governed the universe and women who ruled the world.

The religions of every known early culture were headed by all-woman priesthoods. Her name varied from culture to culture, but in each, She was venerated as the "all-Mother," the "Eternal Great One," the "Immortal Creatress." In all cultures, in every society, her association with the Moon was evident.

In Polynesia the "Creator" of the universe was the Goddess Hina, a word meaning "Moon"; in Finland it was the Creatrix Luonnotar, the "Moon" who breathed life into the World Soul. In other parts of Scandinavia it was Mardoll, the "Moon Shining Over the Sea" who gave birth to the heavens and the Earth.

In ancient Peru it was the Moon-Goddess Mama Quilla who

founded the world, the sacred capital city of Cuzco (the "navel" of the universe), and the Incan people themselves. And in ancient Israel the Sun-God Yahweh was formed, in part, from the Canaanite Moon-Goddess Yareah, whose matrilineal culture and lunar religion permeated every aspect of early Jewish society. To this day the Jewish calendar is still Moon-based and a Jewish identity is still passed down through the maternal side of the family.

Names of locations, too, reflected the Goddess orientation of prehistoric and later ancient people. England, for instance, was once called Albion, the name of the "milk-white" Moon-Goddess; Upper Egypt was originally called Khemennu, the "Land of the Moon"; the continent of Europe was named after the Moon-Goddess Europa ("broad-faced one"); and the country Galatia took its name from the Celtic Moon-Goddess Gala ("milk").

Still today our thinking is imbued with the vestiges of this ancient concept of the synchronistic connection between women's biological make-up and the workings of the Cosmos. What was myth long ago has become a matter of psychoanalysis today. Freud referred to the unconscious as vast and deep: "oceanic." The unconscious is both within us and out of us: it is represented by our oceans but also by our skies. It is below us and above us. And the unconscious is distinctly Feminine.

4

The Story of the Ancient Moon-Goddess Diana

> "They say it is better to be poor and happy than rich and miserable, but how about a compromise like moderately rich and just moody?" —Princess Diana

BY THE TIME THE ROMAN Empire had established itself, one Goddess had ascended into becoming the most powerful Goddess, and it was She who was revered above all others. Diana, whose name can be translated into "Queen of Heaven," reigned supreme. Not only was she the matroness of childbirth, nursing and healing, she was also ruler of the forests, of wild animals, and of the feral nature of humanity. She represented the primordial forces of Nature, the life-loving instinct as well as the death-loving instinct.

Diana was the Sacred Princess of freedom and independence. In ancient Greece she was portrayed as the fiercely independent, completely self-possessed Goddess Artemis. A highly skilled bow-woman, she roamed the forests, avoiding men and shunning marriage. Tied to no man, this matron of sex and reproduction, the Roman Diana, the wild Goddess, answered to no one but herself. (She was the first women's libber.)

Diana's sacred symbol was the sickle-shaped lunar crescent, and at her weekly Sabbath Day temple feast— held on the Moon's sacred day (Moon Day, or "Monday")—devotees honored her name by eating small communion cakes with crosses inscribed on them.

It was this Moon-Goddess, supervisor of the Moon, of the night, the wilderness, and the hunt, who was Diana Spencer's ancient name-sake.

In assuming her position as princess and queen-to-be, the British Diana became for women all around the globe the literal embodiment of a modern day Goddess. It is not surprising then that during the early phase of her marriage to Prince Charles, through to the birth of their two sons, Diana represented an archetype of womanness to so many. On a deep psychic level within us all, she became the very embodiment of womanhood, the personification of the Feminine Principle itself.

The ancient Roman Diana lived in the conscious minds of her devotees. Though she was a creature of mythology, she was as real to them as our own Diana Spencer was to us. The representation of Diana the Moon-Goddess has carried forth from the conscious minds of our early ancestors to the collective unconscious of each individual through the centuries up to the modern world.

Diana the Moon-Goddess exists in the memory of all humans as a collective archetype. It is for this reason, as well as for Diana Spencer's true personality, that she holds such fascination for humanity, and captivated our hearts for the seventeen short years that we knew her.

5

The Sun & the Moon: Balancing the Masculine & Feminine

"Family is the most important thing in the world." — Princess Diana

ANCIENT PEOPLES UNDERSTOOD, LONG BEFORE the science of genetics emerged, that the individual possesses both male and female energies. This understanding dates back to at least the late Neolithic, the period in which the great civilizations of ancient Europe, the Americas, Egypt and Mesopotamia arose.

Though the biologic mechanics of reproduction were not fully understood at this time, with the development of the domestication of wild animals, it finally became plain to Neolithic people that each human being is created out of the mysterious union of a woman—personified in the Moon, and a man—personified in the Sun.

It was only natural that both the Sun and the Moon, with their ever-present luminescence and contrasting aspects, came to most accurately define the principles of Male and Female, even the very act of procreation itself.

Our ancestors understood that the Sun rules the day and the world around us, where things are visible and clear. It gives bountiful light and heats the world with its intense golden fire. It nourishes the plants which in turn feed humanity. Its daily morning appearance and evening disappearance suggested to the ancients the cycle of life and the idea of resurrection. Its orderly and domineering presence seemed "man-like."

These traits, along with its aggressive dry heat, self-generating light, rigid, unchanging shape, and its constant daily and yearly cycles, quite naturally prompted its identification with the Male Principle, with the natural, outer world, with the sky and virility, with fertilization, physical force, knowledge, and with temporal and political power. Thus was born the idea of the male "Sun-God," later transmogrified into the "Son-God."

The Moon, on the other hand, rules the night and the world within as well as the underworld, where vision is murky and smells are dank. The Moon gives a soft, subdued light, and cools the world with its delicate silver glow.

The Moon's ever-changing shape and its relation to various earthly rhythms gives it a "living" presence, and connects it with ideas of change and transformation, with birth and death. Its gentle light is reflective, and it "dies" for three days each month (i.e., goes dark) before its rebirth as the crescent "new Moon." During this phase of rebirth, the Moon's "horns" are sacredly linked to cows. This association spawned the emergence of hundreds of Cow-Goddesses around the world. The sacredness that Hindus hold for their bovines, as well as our own nursery rhyme about the cow jumping over the Moon, are both vestiges of this once popular Pagan figure.

Cow-Goddesses were once numerous and ubiquitous among the various peoples and religions of the world. These included: Amashilamma (Sumerian), Anat (Ugaritic), Audhumbla (Scandinavian), Bo Find (Irish), Glas (Irish), Hathor (Egyptian), Hera (Greek), Mehurt (Egyptian), Neith (Egyptian), Nut (Egyptian), Prithivi (Indian), Sibilja (Swedish), Suki (Indian), Surabhi (Indian), and Tefnut (Egyptian), just to name a few.

Too, the modern sacrality accorded the number three has its origins in the three days in which the Moon "dies." From this single celestial phenomenon derives the concept of the Great Virgin Triple-Goddess, who governed life, death, and the afterlife, and ruled the Moon, the Sun, and the stars—indeed, the entire universe. The Virgin Triple-Goddess bore many names in many different ancient religions, but in the Near and Middle East she was best known as Ma, Ma Ma, Mar, Mara, Marah, Mari, Mariah, Marina, Miryam, or Miriam. In ancient Rome she was called Maria, while in England she appeared in the Robin Hood mythology as Maid Marian.

When Christianity emerged, it adopted Paganism's Virgin Triple-Goddess Maria, christianizing her as the singular "Virgin Mary." But a remnant of the original triplicate Pagan Goddess can still be seen in the Gospel of John where the "Three Marys" gather at the foot of the cross of the Son-God (Sun-God) Jesus (see Jn. 19:25). The book of Revelations too continued to portray the Virgin Mary as a Pagan Goddess, even describing her as riding upon her sacred planetary symbol, the crescent ("horned") Moon, while "clothed with the Sun" and wearing a "crown of twelve stars" (Rev. 12:1).

The Moon's unique characteristics, along with its associations with rain, moistness, darkness, and mystery prompted the ancients to deeply identify it with the Female Principle, the supernatural inner world. This was a world of fecundity and fructification, where reason, wisdom, and eternal spiritual power manifested in the Divine Feminine.

The essential unity of the masculine Sun and the feminine Moon was, for early people, a spiritual idea that was held in very high esteem. And it was not just Pagans who understood this principle. Christians too, like the mystic Saint Francis of Assisi, often spoke and wrote of "Brother Sun" and "Sister Moon."

Just as the Sun and the Moon are both necessary for the balance of all earthly phenomena, the Sun and Moon aspects of each individual and each relationship need to be in balance. This psychic state of balance—the birth-right of each individual—was called "the Meeting of the Sun and Moon."

In ancient times the marriage of the Sun and Moon was the ultimate sanctification of life. It was celebrated in a ritual called *Hieros Gamos*, the "Sacred Union." This merging was thought to be the literal sanctified bonding of God and Goddess, a union that represented spiritual, emotional, and sexual harmony between the Male and Female Principles.

This unity of archetypal Solar (masculine) and Lunar (feminine) traits was believed to exist not only in the greater Cosmos, but in each individual as well. In the world of Goddess, however, the Sun and Moon energies were not specifically tied to Male and Female Principles. The Sun had both Female and Male aspects, as did the Moon. Ideally, there would be a balance of both Sun and Moon in each individual.

The idea of the unification of these two polar energies finds modern validation in the study of depth psychology. Since Freud, all of psychotherapy has had as its goal the rebalancing of the self. From Freud's initial dichotomies between conscious and unconscious, life and death, love and aggression, *eros* and *thanatos*, other psychoanalysts have emphasized the divided self in its various aspects.

The Swiss psychiatrist Carl G. Jung formulated the concepts of *anima* and *animus* (literally, female and male). He identified these aspects as unconscious processes of both males and females: the feminine psychological qualities that a male possesses; and the masculine qualities possessed by the female. The anima development in a male allows him to open up to his emotionality, and in that way a broader spirituality is created that includes intuition, creativity, imagination, and psychic sensitivity towards himself and others where it might not have existed previously.

William R. D. Fairbairn, Scottish physician and psychoanalyst, emphasized the self in contradistinction to the object (ego vs. other); Sybille K. Escalona, American psychoanalytic researcher, referred to the initial symbiosis and subsequent individuation (fusion and separation). Each of these psychoanalytic formulations is merely a modern version of the ancient *Hieros Gamos*, the Meeting of the Sun and Moon.

We yearn to be whole, and we yearn to be made whole in our relationships. Without such balanced wholeness, without all of our aspects being allowed manifestation, we will feel neither comfortable, nor familiar with the worlds in which we live, both our inner world wherein reside our thoughts and feelings, and the outer world surrounding us, wherein reside our behaviors and activities.

When we perceive the union between Diana and Charles as a modern day representation of this ancient but universal emblem of the *Hieros Gamos*, we can then understand why their marriage became an international sensation. On a collective unconscious level, people from nearly every country on Earth, from every walk of life, reverberated in harmony with the inner Solar-Lunar meaning of Diana and Charles' panoptic tale of public power (Sun) and personal romance (Moon).

Just as our modern Diana embodied the Feminine, Charles personified the basic traits of manhood. During his courtship and early marriage to Diana, with his noble bearing and love of horses, he reminded us of a proud knight on his silver charger.

Indeed, as Diana's very name suggests the Feminine, the name Charles, on the other hand, means literally "manly." Like Diana, Charles, as King-to-be, ruler of the land, represents an ancient and universal archetype: the Sun-God or Sun-King in human form, the male counterpart to the feminine Moon-Goddess or Moon-Queen.

In the collective psyche then, Diana epitomized for all of us the Female Moon Principle (anima), while Charles embodied the Male Sun Principle (animus). In the collective unconscious we all resonated with Diana as Female: soft, subtle, sensual and ever-changing, and with Charles as Male: tough, gregarious, stoic and constant. Early in their marriage we had every reason to believe that their union would be as perfect and harmonious as the ancient rite of the Sacred Union of the Sun and Moon.

6

The Cosmic Split: Diana & Charles' Divorce

"I don't want expensive gifts; I don't want to be bought. I have everything I want. I just want someone to be there for me, to make me feel safe and secure." — Princess Diana

DIANA, AS WELL AS BEING a symbol for all women, was very much a woman of her times. When we see early images of her we see a woman, an ingénue of a woman, looking at her husband with doe-eyes, young, naive and innocent. We see from these photos that she was frequently looking up at him rather than across to him eye-to-eye.

And we were witness to her attraction to him, the masculinity and strength which she believed was basic to who he was. Early in their relationship, she was the princess, a maiden-in-waiting, deferent and obliging to her man. We do not yet see her knowing her own strength as a woman. She has not yet matured into her own inner Moon-Goddess, Diana, ruler of the world, Mother to all.

Ironically, the very force that drew Diana and Charles together in the beginning later pulled them apart. What was this mysterious energy that was so powerful that it not only magnetized two individuals from completely different worlds, but later split them asunder? It was precisely Charles' Sun energy and Diana's Moon energy.

Acting as complimentary forces, Diana's Moon at first hoped to dance in the outpouring light of Charles' brilliant Sun. At the same time Charles' Sun wished to bathe in the reflected light of Diana's soft Moon. Yet, while their beginning seemed promising, ultimately Charles the Sun and Diana the Moon did not merge into a harmonious marriage of opposites. What happened?

Imagine Diana's surprise when only a few years into the marriage she discovered that Charles' Sun only comes out in public, and that in his day-to-day life he was actually a shy, introspective Moon. His preference for quiet reflection was far stronger than his desire for noisy society. In fact, Charles' favorite pastime was, and remains, haunting stark Scottish heaths, where he can engage in watercolor painting in complete solitude.

Too, Charles spent as much time thinking about the past as Diana did living in the present. Particularly interested in ecology, organic foods, and classic architecture, he despised modernism in all its forms. "When he's home all he does is retreat behind an emotional cloud," Diana might have mused to herself in dissatisfaction with her husband's brooding, dark Moon energy.

On the other hand, we can imagine Charles' shock when, for the first time, he realized that Diana's Moon was only a public facade, and that in her everyday life she was actually a boisterous, mischievous, attention-loving Sun. As much as Charles hated the social whirlwind, Diana hated being alone. She loved everything about the contemporary world, was unabashedly materialistic, and had little or no interest in the historical past.

Instead, she loved the here and now, and most especially people living in the here and now. Hence, she devoted herself tirelessly to charity work and to those less fortunate. "She's so sociable and outgoing, it's hard to hear oneself think around her," Charles must have muttered to himself in dissatisfaction with his wife's Sun energy.

Diana tried as long as she could to suppress her frustration and disappointment at her discovery of Charles' true self. But her stronger Solar side came out and in typical Sun fashion she turned her anger outward onto her husband. In public, she pouted, cried, and sulked. In private she turned this anger against herself. Friends spoke of suicide attempts, putting her hand through a glass case, and purposefully throwing herself down a long flight of stairs.

All of this was calculated to show the world, and to prove to herself, that it was Charles who was the sole cause of her misery. Diana, in this state, shows the Sun energy at its worst: overly dramatic, self-centered, hypercritical, irrational.

As for Charles, his strongest side is Lunar. And like a typical Moon he withdrew inward. In public, he steeled his emotions against Diana's behavior by cloaking himself in an air of cool detachment. Gone were the warm smiles, the playful jests at Diana, the friendly waving at fans from the back seat of his limousine. All we saw was the cold exterior of an anguished man. In private, he retreated to his former relationship with Camille Parker-Bowles (née Shand),[1] where he could still experience himself as strong and desirable. Charles, in this state, shows the Moon in its weakest light: pallid, insipid, frigid, untrustworthy, aloof.

At last, invariably, the tension between the two became too great and this Marriage of the Sun and Moon, this regal Sacred Union, ended in rupture: bitterness and separation and, finally, divorce.

Perhaps Diana and Charles might have been helped if they had had a grasp of archetypal psychology. Perhaps they would have done better if they had understood that the opposing Solar and Lunar energies need to be harmonized, not only with one another in relationships, but within themselves as individuals.

In great part, it was the royal couple's unawareness of these basic concepts—and their inability to put into practice the implications of these concepts—that finally ended their Sacred Union.

---

1. As he was with Princess Diana, Charles and Camilla are cousins.

7

Lunar Phases of the Goddess: Diana's Transformation

"I like to be a free spirit. Some don't like that,
but that's the way I am." — Princess Diana

EVEN BEFORE HER DIVORCE FROM Charles, Diana had
come to accept that she was in a loveless marriage, plunging
her into deep despair. This was the period of her bulemia
and her ill-fated affair with a polo player who sold her out for a
story. But she rallied—emotionally and spiritually—and began a
transformative process that took her in the direction of the Goddess
who ruled her.

Diana's identification with the unloved and unwanted led her to go
out among the peoples of the earth and touch society's outcasts. In
her acts of charity, her travels to the dark "underworld," her
willingness to enter places where fear and morbidity
predominate—that is, the places of the Moon-Goddess—and in her

desire to bring healing to these places, she began to truly embody the Moon-Mother-Goddess.

Too, through Diana's struggles to find herself and her strength, she never forgot her maternal obligations to her two boys, Prince William and Prince Harry. They were, above all, her life and her commitment. This is Goddess at her best, her unswerving devotion to the nurturance of her own off-spring, as well as all of Earth's children.

This universal passion for humanity is indeed an archetypal trait of the Moon-Mother-Goddess who, at the creation of the universe, poured her love out across the night sky in the form of breast milk. To this day we still call this band of light in the heavens the "Milky Way," which, as a scientific phenomenon, is actually a side view of what we still revealingly refer to as the "Galaxy." The word Galaxy derives from the name of the Greek Moon-Goddess Gala (meaning "milk") and also the Latin word *lac* ("milk)." Galaxy then (like the word Ga-lactic) literally means the "milk of the Moon-Goddess."

Diana herself, the modern day Moon-Goddess, was aware of her transformation. She was quoted as saying that she intended to change her life. Only weeks before she died, she auctioned off many of her most expensive gowns and donated the proceeds to charity. It was as though by shedding her old clothing, she was shedding her "old skin," preparing herself for a new life of freedom and growth.

The transformation that Diana underwent was, in fact, a rebalancing of her Moon and Sun energies. Diana wanted to reclaim her prerogative to live in balance with both Sun and Moon aspects. She wanted to live in the territory of the Sun, to have the Sun's loud authoritative voice as well as the Moon's soft reflective one.

She wished to share the Sun's brilliant light of world events as well as staying in the more subdued Moon shadows of the home and raising her sons; she sought to have the Sun power that financial independence would afford her, as well as having a Moon-like reliance on friends and family.

Diana, like all modern women, wanted to be both a Sun and a Moon, and she came to understand that the healing of all of us, including our non-human compatriots on this earth (animals), and the living organism of the Earth itself, would be influenced by her success.

Curiously, Diana's inner Goddess journey was mirrored in actual human history.

8

The Patriarchal Takeover: Rise & Fall of the Matriarchate

"I think the biggest disease the world suffers from in this day and age is the disease of people feeling unloved. I know that I can give love for a minute, for half an hour, for a day, for a month, but I can give. I am very happy to do that, I want to do that." — Princess Diana

JUST AS DIANA'S MARRIAGE BEGAN to crumble under the stresses of her life as a royal in Britain's patriarchal monarchy, around 4300 B.C.E. the Matriarchate began to dissolve under the pressures of what has been called the "Patriarchal Takeover." Tragically, during the rise to power of ancient Greece, the idea that only men should be Suns (masculine) and only women should be Moons (feminine) began to be promulgated around the world.

In Europe specifically the Matriarchy first started to collapse when horseback riding tribes came in from the east—from the area of the Black Sea (bound by present-day southeastern Europe, Russia, and Turkey)—and began to wrestle positions of power away from women. In the process the casual, religion-based matriarchies of the Goddess World were transformed into formal, military-based patriarchies of the God World.

By 1400 B.C.E., this patriarchal tidal wave had reached Egypt, where the nation's many Moon-Goddesses were dethroned, replaced by a singular Sun-God known as Aten ("All-Father"), one of the precursors of the monotheistic Jewish Sun-God Yahweh. In Greece the Moon-Goddesses were ousted and replaced by the Sun-God Zeus ("Bright Sky"), while in Rome it was the Sun-God Jupiter ("God-Father") who took the throne.

And so the old Moon-Goddess was supplanted by the new Sun-God; the original Mother-Earth-Goddess was superseded by the foreign Father-Sky-God; and theacracy (a goddess-based government) was replaced by something entirely new: theocracy (a god-based government).

The "Great Mother" was not only overturned, but her teachings were repressed. The newly established patriarchies had little respect for women, their female Supreme Being, for Goddess' sacred symbols, or for her followers. As just as few examples: the word men, which originally meant "Moon," and by extension "women," was transformed by the new patriarchies into a word meaning "male."

The number 13, both the number of months in Goddess' lunar year and the number of a woman's yearly menstrual cycles (and thus Goddess' sacred number), was depicted as "unlucky." The number 13 could not even be spoken, a patriarchal fear which later, in more modern times, gave rise to such phrases as "a baker's dozen" and the removal of the number 13 on the thirteenth floor of buildings.

The holy blessing of the Moon-Goddess, known as being "Moon-struck," was changed to the negative, to mean "one who has been struck dumb." A "lunatic," originally a respected member of Goddess' lunar religion, was altered to denote a "crazy person." Members of the religion of the Moon-Goddess Selene ("Moon") were specifically selected for ridicule by the new patriarchies: it is from Selene's name that we get the word "silly."

The name of the Moon-God Sin—who ruled the ancient Egyptian city of Sin (Eze. 30:15-16), Mt. Sinai and the Sinai Peninsula—was transferred from a name of holiness associated with Goddess, to one indicating iniquity, evil and immorality; hence, our modern word "sin."

The militant Romans, under Emperor Julian, even threw out the Goddess' 13-month lunar menstrual calendar which reckoned the day from noon to noon. In its place they instituted the 12-month solar calendar which illogically reckons the day from midnight to midnight. Goddess' New Year's Day, which naturally fell on the first day of Spring (March 21) was irrationally altered to fall in mid-Winter (January 1), forever mangling the Western calendar: as the original Latin meaning of their names indicate, September ("seventh month"), October ("eighth month"), November ("ninth month"), and December ("tenth month"), were once part of the Pagan Calendar, which began each year on the Spring Equinox (March 21).

The patriarchal conquest of the Goddess World also called for a change in the Sabbath Day. The new patriarchies, in keeping with their exclusive worship of the Sun, changed the Sabbath from Moon Day ("Monday") and replaced it with the day which honored the "Almighty Sun-God," the first day of the week, Sun Day ("Sunday"). With this new emphasis on Sun worship rather than Moon worship, the "followers of the Left-Hand Path," as Goddess' devotees called themselves (after the direction the Moon travels in), were substituted by the "followers of the Right-Hand Path" (the direction the Sun travels in).

For 5,000 years, we have been living with the after-math of the Patriarchal Takeover. Its legacy has been a culture that is patriarchal, male-oriented, and female-loathing; one that functions around the idea of domination. Today not only are there no women-only societies, religions, or governments as there once had been around the globe, but in many contemporary cultures women are still not even allowed to serve in political or religious offices.

The last real remnant of the Goddess World is to be found in what is now deprecatingly called "Witchcraft," or Wicca, as it is more correctly known by its practitioners, a benign, Nature-worshiping religion with Goddess and her male consort at its center (note that Wiccans do not believe in Satan or the Devil).

Menelaus.   Paris.   Diomedes.   Odisseus.   Nestor.   Achilles.   Agamemnon.

Sadly, the all-female matriarchies, with their cooperative societies and reciprocal (bartering) economies, have utterly vanished, replaced by all-male patriarchies which rule by hierarchical government and function under a commercial market economy.

Furthermore, all women today are forced to claim citizenship in male-dominated nations, and must belong to male-created religions that serve mainly masculine gods.

Judaism and Christianity, once female-centered,[2] are now wholly male-centered and serve only masculine gods. And while women's ability to procreate is emphasized (mainly to increase the faith's membership), her intellectual and athletic abilities are largely disregarded.

Also at odds with the former roles of women is the fact that today most women take the last names of their male counterparts and name their children after them, customs that would have been considered blasphemous in early Goddess societies.

In particular, our American culture, like the British culture from which we originally derived, is a Sun-oriented tradition. We value, seemingly above all else, power and materialism. Our American Sun-tradition even replaced a Moon culture, the Amerindians, who like the ancient Cretans, lived in harmony with Nature, were spiritual and egalitarian, and worshiped a female Supreme Being.

---

2. See, for example, Ge. 2:24; Ge. 36:1-5; Je. 44:15-25; Je. 31:22; De. 23:18; Is. 3:12; Job 1:15; 1 K. 1:1-5; 1 K. 11:5, 31-33; 1 K. 15:13; 2 K. 11:3; Ps. 48:3; Mt. 12:42; Jn. 19:25; Jn. 20:11-18; Acts 19: 24-37).

9

Amulets & Croissants:
Survivals of the Matriarchate

"People think at the end of the day that a man
is the only answer to fulfillment. Actually a
job is better for me." — Princess Diana

THE NEW PATRIARCHATE WENT TO enormous
lengths to obliterate the old Matriarchate, particularly
among Jews and Christians, two religions whose origins
were firmly rooted in far older Pagan Goddess traditions. Despite
thousands of years of violent
suppression, however, vestiges of the
ancient Goddess world survived, not
only in ancient times, but right into the
present day.

For example, although the all-male
priesthood of ancient Judaism
attempted to pass into law anti-Goddess
sentiment, saying "thou shalt not suffer
a witch to live" (Ex. 22:18), they were
not entirely successful: the great

Hebrew King Saul ignored the order and consulted a Moon-priestess at Endor (1 S. 28:6-20).

Goddess-worship survived in other aspects of Judaism as well. The ancient Jewish "Ark of the Covenant" was actually a sickle-shaped box patterned on the crescent Moon-Boat, a fertility symbol representing the sacred vulva (Jos. 3:6). Goddess-worship itself continued in practice until Isaiah's time: Jewish women at the time disregarded prohibitions against female religion and honored their own Moon-Mother-Goddess, Ashtoreth (1 K. 11:33), by wearing her sacred symbol, the Lunar crescent, in the form of amulets (Is. 3:18).

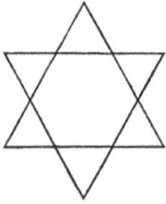

Goddess-worshiping Jews continued to promote and develop their secret faith as late as the Seventeenth Century, when mainstream Judaism adopted the Pagan hexagram as its emblem. Now known by the patriarchal name the "Star of David," the Jewish hexagram, with its interlocking triangles (the male triangle pointing up, the female triangle pointing down), is an overt copy of the original Pagan hexagram, used throughout prehistory to symbolize the mystical Union of the Female and Male Principles.

The Latin cross, used by the Christian faith, also shows remnants of the Great Goddess Religion. The emblem is found in the cave art of the Cro-Magnon people who flourished some 35,000 years ago. The horizontal beam symbolizes the Female Principle, which is perforated by the vertical beam, a symbol of the Male Principle.

The cross was originally so identified with Goddess Religion that the Christian Fathers prohibited its use. Thus the earliest artistic and literary representations of Jesus portray him

hanging not on a cross, but on a tree, an image that is still found in some of the oldest books of the New Testament.[3]

Even after centuries of attempting to drive the Female Principle underground, survivals of the Goddess era—when the Female reigned supreme, when Diana the Moon-Goddess held court over every land—remain even in the modern era.

For instance, some modern Christian groups, sects, and denominations, such as the Shakers, Rosicrucians, Gnostics, Freemasons, Christian Scientists, and Mormons (LDS), continue the tradition of Mother-Goddess-worship in one form or another. The word *croissant* (the French word for "crescent") is a leftover of the sickle-shaped Eucharistic cakes used by Moon-Goddess religions in their sacraments (to this day, the colloquial term for the croissant is "Moon-teeth").

In the United States an enormous statue of Goddess in New York Harbor continues to protect our shores under one of her contemporary names: "Liberty." But this is an Americanization: in France, where she was originally conceived and constructed, she was known as the ancient Roman Goddess *Libertas*, who governed freedom and emancipation.

The tradition of giving boats and ships women's names reflects the once widespread belief that water was an embodiment of Goddess, and "ladies first" still holds true in all civilized nations. The natural

---

3. See, for example, Acts 5:30; 10:39; 13:29; Ga. 3:13; 1 Pe. 2:24.

world is still referred to in the ancient Goddess manner as "Mother Nature," and the common phrase for one's native land is the "mother-country," a vestige from the time when Goddess ruled entire continents. Indeed countless nations and continents were named after Goddess. Among them: Europe, Africa, China, Scandinavia, Britain, Ireland, Italy, Crete, Scotland, Greece, Romania, Albania, Holland, Denmark, and Israel.

Despite these overt modern survivals of the prehistoric Matriarchate, the new Patriarchate continues to deliver serious blows to the power of the Female. The world Diana Spencer was born into still allows clitorectomies (in many non-Western societies, some in which the procedure is considered "routine," an estimated 100 million women have forcibly undergone the operation); women are still stoned to death in parts of Arabia for adultery; and female newborns are regularly murdered in China.

In the U.S., the most advanced country in the world for women's rights, even the most highly educated women are still paid $.77 for every dollar that their male counterparts make. Female slavery is even still practiced in the U.S.: according to the C.I.A., "as many as 50,000 women and children from Asia, Latin America and Eastern Europe are brought to the United States under false pretenses each year and forced to work as prostitutes, abused laborers, or servants."

The harsh reality is that all over the world misogynism still reigns.

But hatred of the Female manifests in other ways as well. Much of humanity continues to dishonor Goddess in our abuse of Mother Earth. We have paved over her meadows, drained her marshlands, burned down her forests, dynamited her mountains, and killed off her non-human animal children for medical experiments. Many in the Goddess Reclamation Movement attribute this to our worship of the Patriarchal values of power, materialism, and money.

Not only has there been a tragic split between the masculine and feminine sides of our very humanity on a collective level, but each of us individually experiences this rupture on the deepest level of the human psyche. Highlighting this loss has been, as mentioned, Freud's articulation of the unconscious and Jung's postulation of anima and animus, concepts which bring back memory of those long-ago days when balance between Male and Female, Sun and Moon, still permeated people's lives.

Freud and Jung allowed us to see, once again, the life-giving nature of the subtle energy of the Female Principle. They even outlined, with unparalleled precision, the dark implications of turning away from our Feminine-Moon aspects. It is precisely this turning away from hidden aspects of oneself that creates all the varied neurotic ills. Jung defined neurosis as "a breach between the anima and animus." Diana and Charles' marriage itself was a very real symbol of this breach, when the anima (Moon) and animus (Sun) are separated and lose the ability to harmoniously interact, interface and intertwine within one another—both within a relationship and within oneself.

The famous 1723 painting, *Diana and Her Nymphs Bathing*, by Jean-François de Troy. The artist has correctly placed a lunar crescent tiara on the Goddess.

10

Transfiguration of the Moon-Goddess: Diana's Death

"Nothing brings me more happiness than trying to help the most vulnerable people in society. It is a goal and an essential part of my life—a kind of destiny. Whoever is in distress can call on me. I will come running wherever they are." — Princess Diana

THOUSANDS OF YEARS AFTER THE Patriarchal Takeover, when Diana Spencer ascended to her place next to Charles, the future-King, most of us had forgotten our feminine origins. The Princess, like the rest of humanity, had lost sight of the balance of energies that had once personified the ancient Goddess and her world. And little wonder.

Diana had been raised in a patriarchal home (*patrilocality*) where she took her father's last name (*patronymy*), embraced a patriarchal man in a monogamous union (*patriarchal marriage*), took her husband's name (*double patronymy*), moved into her husband's home (*double patrilocality*), and gave birth to two male heirs to carry on the family name (*patriliny*). Naturally all of these patriarchal emphases tended to thwart Diana's inner Goddess, bringing her psychic Moon into conflict with her psychic Sun.

Although she had made many changes before and subsequent to her divorce, by the evening of August 31, 1997, her transformation was not yet complete.

That night, as Diana's car came barreling down a Parisian street to meet her date with destiny, she left her seat-belt undone, something completely out of character for the normally ultra safety-conscious royal. In this instant she gave herself over entirely to our patriarchal society, losing her emerging connection to her own inner Goddess: Diana, the proud and fierce huntress through which she had once walked independently, fearing and needing no man.

And yet Diana Spencer Windsor had quite willingly climbed into a two-ton phallic symbol controlled by three males. She had consented to be led by the hand of a man who had been drinking and who thrilled to danger, high speed, and the chase. These are machismo acts, the Male Principle at its most reckless.

A few hours later, at 12:30 AM, September 1, Diana's speeding Mercedes Benz penetrated a vulva-like tunnel and impaled itself on an erect pillar of cement, a crash that would result in the deaths of three of its four occupants, including the Princess herself.

Diana did not die instantly.

As she lay amid the smoldering ruins of the luxury automobile, with a deep gash in her forehead, strangely she refused all medical treatment. Her final words, a solemn ode to the Patriarchy, were "My God!"

In the height of cosmic synchronicity, the pillar Diana's car struck was the thirteenth column in the tunnel. We will recall that the number thirteen was designated as being one of the most magical numbers of the ancient Moon-Goddess. The French tunnel itself was (and still is) named *Pont de l'Alma*: "Bridge of (the Moon-Goddess) Alma," a fitting title for the portal-like roadway that would carry the Princess into the next world.

Three hours later, at 3:30 AM, at Paris' *Hospital de la Pitie Salpetriere*, Diana the modern day Moon-Goddess, waxed into her final lunar phase: death. She came to her end betrayed and finally crushed by the Patriarchy, a social form epitomized in modern technology, commerce, aggression, speed, and greed.

The hospital in which Diana drew her last breath was first constructed as a storehouse for military weapons. The name *Hospital de la Pitie Salpetriere* hints at its original purpose: at the time, saltpeter was used to make gun powder, an archetypal symbol of the bellicose Patriarchy.

But it was the building's later usage that proved to be the last strange twist in Diana's brief earthly sojourn. In the Seventeenth Century, long before it was turned into a modern hospital, King Louis the XIV had the arsenal renovated into a house for beggars, the poor, the homeless, prostitutes, and former criminals, just the sort of people that Diana Spencer the Moon-Queen so loved to nurture. And, in yet another unnerving irony, Louis the XIV, himself a relative of the princess, was often referred to during his life as the "Sun-King."

Even in its 1997 guise as the *Hospital de la Pitie Salpetriere*, the former weapons storehouse was filled with the innocent, the helpless, the sick, the elderly, all those who Diana most closely related to. If only she could have reached out from her deathbed and given them all one final "royal touch."

But such was not to be. As if to salute Diana's Moon goodbye one last time as it disappeared beneath the penetrating solar rays of the Patriarchy, Diana, the woman, expired at the *Hospital de la Pitie Salpetriere*, the place where she was, finally, most at home.

Her burial on an island in the middle of a small English lake, known as The Round Oval—located on the grounds of Althorp Park (the Spencer family home at Great Brington)—surely befits a modern day Moon-Goddess. It reminds us of the ancient British tale in which a mortally injured King Arthur is rowed to the misty isle of Avalon by nine sister-Goddesses, where he is nursed back to health by their tender ministrations.

Avalon appears in Celtic myth as an earthly paradise where all is perfection and everyday is spring, ruled over by the Moon-Goddess Morgan Le Fay and her eight sisters. The oval is an archetypal Goddess symbol of pregnancy and fructification (still seen in our Easter egg, Easter being a "Christian" holiday based on the old matriarchal Lunar Calendar, and named after the Anglo-Saxon Spring-Goddess Eostre; i.e., "estrus"). In death Diana Spencer retained even these mythic elements.

Nine is a holy Goddess power number because it is the sum of three times three (i.e., the Triple-Goddess tripled), and because it accords with the nine months of pregnancy. Diana was thirty-six at the time of her death, which in sacred numerology equals the number nine (three + six = nine). Thus thirty-six is the number of oak trees (symbol of the Sun/Son-God) which line the path to

Diana's island grave in the Oval, the final resting place of our own modern day Moon-Goddess, one of whose royal titles was "Lady of the Isles."

Finally, in keeping with her favorite flower, the Princess' memorial is surrounded with white roses, a lasting homage to both the modern Diana and the ancient Diana, for the rose is Goddess' most sacred plant, archetypal symbol of the magical life-giving female pudendum.

White is the color of the Moon *and* the age-old symbol of purity and innocence. As such, the white rose is one of the many emblems of the Virgin Mary, often known as "the Mystical Rose of Heaven"—a title borrowed from the far older Pagan female deity, the White-Goddess Europa, once worshiped across the continent which took her name: Europe.

Europa was known throughout the Roman Empire as the Moon-Goddess Diana, one of whose titles, like the Virgin Mary's, was "Queen of Heaven."

Lady Diana Spencer was not Queen of Heaven of course. And she left both her marriage and the world long before she could have become queen of England. But she was, and will always remain, "the queen of people's hearts," the title she herself wanted to be known by.

Epilogue

"I'm aware that people I have loved and have died and are in the spirit world looking after me." — Princess Diana

SOME 2,000 YEARS AGO THE cult of Diana the Moon-Goddess, the archetypal "Lunar Virgin," reached its zenith in the Greco-Roman world. Known in Greece as Artemis the "Great Huntress" and the "Mother of Wild Animals," she was worshiped everywhere as the original Notre Dame ("Our Lady"), the universal Pagan Madonna of the ancient Mediterranean region.

So popular was Diana's religion at the time that orthodox Christian authorities viewed her as a threat to their own Goddess, Mary the mother of Jesus. Church officials began calling for the Pagan deity's temples to be pulled down, saying that she should be "despised" and "her magnificence should be destroyed." A frustrated Saint Paul once complained of "the great goddess Diana, whom all Asia and the world worshippeth."[4]

Since the Moon-Goddess is an archetype, and hence can never be truly "destroyed," after banning Paganism the Church had no choice but to simply assimilate her—the usual resolution to this all too

---

4. Ac. 19:27.

common Pagan "problem." Di-Ana (that is, the "Goddess Ana") became "Anna," the mother of Mary, while Mary herself was proclaimed a "virgin," portrayed just like the Pagan Goddess, with a crescent "moon under her feet."[5]

After Diana's temples were torn down, Christian churches were built over the old sites. Diana's name was purged from the history books, her memory slandered, her figure damned to an eternal hell of fire and brimstone. One would assume that the Great Virgin-Lunar-Goddess was now forever dead and gone.

But such was not the case.

Despite the Church's best efforts to obliterate her, the cult of Diana lived on; not just in the overt and public veneration of the Virgin Mary and Anna the "Grandmother of God," but also in the underground world of secret societies, occult organizations, and clandestine "unorthodox" religions, where, into the present, she has remained the much revered Queen of Heaven, the Triple-Goddess of birth, life, and death.

Twenty centuries passed. Then came a day that will live forever in

---

5. Rev. 12:1.

our memories: July 1, 1961. Though unbeknownst to all those involved, it was on this particular day that the cult of Diana would become renewed via a rather seemingly unremarkable event: the birth, at Park House (Sandringham Estate), of Diana Frances Spencer (to Edward John Spencer and Frances Ruth Burke Roche) under the astrological sign Cancer—*which is ruled by the Moon.*

As we have seen, Diana's life and death indeed closely echoed the lunarian sign she was born in, as well as the Moon-Goddess she was named after. She was, as Cancerians are quite properly called, a true "Moon-child" in every sense of the phrase. Though in her case she was not only a child of Luna, she literally grew into a goddess herself, what we in the 21st Century call a "celebrity."

Althorp, the Spencer family home

Her mortal wounding in a Parisian tunnel discloses other uncanny synchronicities: known as the "Bridge of Alma," in ancient times it was the site of a famed Goddess Temple, where Pagans sacrificed to their great female deity. What was her name? *Alma* is Latin for "nurturing," that is, nurse-like, which describes the Great Mother-Goddess, who, like the Princess of Wales, was kind and indulgent to everyone.

In Spanish (along with Latin, a member of the Italic branch of Indo-European languages) *alma* means "soul," and in most languages the word for soul is feminine, as the ancients perceived the Spirit or Holy Spirit (symbolized in Christian myth as a dove) as female. One's "alma mater" is thus one's "soul mother." *Alma* in turn has associations with the Latin word *alba*, "white," the color of the Moon.

In Hebrew *almah* means a "young woman," which Christians translate as "virgin,"[6] while across the ancient Middle East *Al-Mah* (mystically, "All Mother") was once another name for the universal Lunar-Goddess. Diana Spencer died on August 1, 1997, under the sign of Leo, ruled by the planetary symbol of the Patriarchy, the Sun, *Sol*, whose wife was known as *Luna* the "Virgin"—one of the many titles of the Moon-Goddess whose very name she received: Diana.

---

6. See Is. 7:14; Mt: 1:23.

The Princess' family was certainly aware of at least some of these strange connections between the Goddess Diana and the woman Diana, for after her death her brother Earl Spencer made reference to the ancient Moon-Goddess in a public speech regarding Lady Di's life.

Society is also cognizant, though unconsciously, of these mystical relationships between the two archetypal females, one mythical, the other historical. This is why today, after all, the cult of Diana Spencer is more popular, more vital, more widespread than ever. Dozens of new Lady Di fan clubs continue to sprout up each year, while social media alone boasts several thousand sites dedicated to the "People's Princess." Private businesses that have named themselves after her (such as London's popular "Café Diana"), compete with a host of both private and government sponsored memorial parks, fountains, and statues that annually appear in her honor in cities all over the world.

Untold thousands visit her grave site at Althorp Park, where a Paganesque stone temple and wilderness shrine (both befitting the ancient Goddess as well) have been erected, while in London, along the famous "Diana, Princess of Wales Memorial Walk," there are 90 beautiful plaques sporting the Pagan five-petaled rose of the old Moon-Goddess.

Even here we cannot escape the ties that bind our modern day Moon-Goddess to the ancient one. Numerologically 90 reduces to nine, a triplicate of the Triple-Goddess (another name for Diana or Artemis), while five, due to its association with the shape of a human being (with arms and legs outstretched), is the sacred number of humanity, familiarly seen in the starry symbol known as the pentacle.

Goddess Diana's crown, with the lunar crescent in the middle, is actually a tiara comprised of twelve stars symbolizing the twelve signs of the Zodiac, which in turn represent spiritual perfection by way of the twelve human faculties or soul qualities: 1) love, 2) faith, 3) strength, 4) judgment, 5) understanding, 6) self-control, 7) power, 8) will, 9) imagination, 10) fervor, 11) orderliness, and 12) acquisitiveness.[7] And so the Virgin Mary too was later depicted standing upon a crescent Moon wearing "upon her head a crown of twelve stars."[8]

Like the Moon itself, Diana Spencer has come full circle through the three great lunar phases: birth, life, and death. Yet, she has been resurrected once again as the "New Moon" in the archetype of her early Roman namesake.

While alive Princess Diana was indeed like our Moon in the sky: we knew she was there, believed she would always be there. We watched her movements with fascination and admiration. We

---

7. Twelve became sacred in prehistoric times due to its easy divisibility: it can be divided into twos, threes, fours, and sixes. Thus we have the Twelve Apostles of Mithras, the Twelve Sons of Odin, the Twelve Knights of the Roundtable, the Twelve Disciples of Buddha, the Twelve Labors of Hercules, the Twelve Peers of Roland, the Twelve Days of Christmas, the Twelve Tribes of Israel, the Twelve Apostles of Jesus, etc.

8. Rev. 12:1.

never imagined a world without her any more than we imagine a world without our Moon.

The world has mourned Diana's loss like no other. At the time of her death, women despaired and were devastated over the tragic loss. It was a loss that many women felt on an intensely personal level—as though they knew her, as though she had been a valued best friend, even a treasured family member.

Every day that we wake up now, without Diana's presence on this earth, we feel like we have lost something irreplaceable, something as valuable, as crucial to us as our Moon.

And yet, just as the Patriarchy has not been able to kill off the Goddess, the Feminine archetype which Diana embodied also lives on. Not in the conscious mind ruled by the Male, but in the unconscious mind, ruled by the Female—abode of the world heart-soul, the true essence of both the Moon-Goddess and the Moon-child.

Appendix A

PRINCESS DIANA

"Any sane person would have left long ago. But I cannot. I have my sons."

"Being a princess isn't all it's cracked up to be."

"Carry out a random act of kindness, with no expectation of reward, safe in the knowledge that one day someone might do the same for you."

"Every one of us needs to show how much we care for each other and, in the process, care for ourselves."

"HIV does not make people dangerous to know, so you can shake their hands and give them a hug: Heaven knows they need it."

"Hugs can do great amounts of good—especially for children."

"I don't even know how to use a parking meter, let alone a phone box."

"I knew what my job was; it was to go out and meet the people and love them."

"I live for my sons. I would be lost without them."

"I think like any marriage, especially when you've had divorced parents like myself; you want to try even harder to make it work."

"I want my boys to have an understanding of people's emotions, their insecurities, people's distress, and their hopes and dreams."

"I want to walk into a room, be it a hospital for the dying or a hospital for the sick children, and feel that I am needed. I want to do, not just to be."

"I wear my heart on my sleeve."

"I will fight for my children on any level so they can reach their potential as human beings and in their public duties."

"I'm as thick as a plank."

"The greatest problem in the world today is intolerance. Everyone is so intolerant of each other."

"If men had to have babies, they would only ever have one each."

"If you find someone you love in your life, then hang on to that love."

"It's vital that the monarchy keeps in touch with the people. It's what I try and do."

"Only do what your heart tells you."

"So many people supported me through my public life and I will never forget them."

"The biggest disease this day and age is that of people feeling unloved."

"The kindness and affection from the public have carried me through some of the most difficult periods, and always your love and affection have eased the journey."

"When you are happy you can forgive a great deal."

"You can't comfort the afflicted with afflicting the comfortable."

"What must it be like for a little boy to read that daddy never loved mummy?"

Bibliography

Allen, Paula Gunn. *The Sacred Hoop: Recovering the Feminine in American Indian Traditions*. Boston, MA: Beacon Press, 1986.

Ames, Winthrop (ed.). *What Shall We Name the Baby?* 1941. New York, NY: Pocket Books, 1974 ed.

Andrews, George C. *Extra-Terrestrials Among Us*. 1986. St. Paul, MN: Llewellyn, 1993 ed.

Andrews, Ted. *The Occult Christ: Angelic Mysteries, Seasonal Rituals, and The Divine Feminine*. St. Paul, MN: Llewellyn, 1993.

Angus, Samuel. *The Mystery-Religions and Christianity: A Study of the Religious Background of Early Christianity*. 1925. New York, NY: Citadel Press, 1966 ed.

Armstrong, Karen. *A History of God: The 4000-Year Quest of Judaism, Christianity and Islam*. New York, NY: Knopf, 1993.

Ashe, Geoffrey. *The Virgin: Mary's Cult and the Re-emergence of the Goddess*. 1976. London, UK: Arkana, 1988 ed.

——. *Dawn Behind the Dawn: A Search for the Earthly Paradise*. New York, NY: Holt, 1992.

Attwater, Donald. *The Penguin Dictionary of Saints*. 1965. Harmondsworth, UK: Penguin (second edition revised by Catherine Rachel John), 1983 ed.

Ayto, John. *Dictionary of Word Origins*. New York, NY: Arcade, 1990.

Bailey, Sandra Buzbee. *Big Book of Baby Names*. Tucson, AZ: HP

Books, 1982.

Barnstone, Willis (ed.). *The Other Bible: Ancient Esoteric Texts.* New York, NY: Harper and Row, 1984.

Baring, Anne, and Jules Cashford. *The Myth of the Goddess: Evolution of an Image.* 1991. Harmondsworth, UK: Arkana, 1993 ed.

Baumgartner, Anne S. *A Comprehensive Dictionary of the Gods: From Abaasy to Zvoruna.* New York, NY: University Books, 1984.

Bede. *Historia Ecclesiastica Gentis Anglorum* (*A History of the English Church and People*, Leo Sherley-Price, trans.). C.E. 731. Harmondsworth, UK: Penguin, 1955 (1974 ed.).

Begg, Ean. *The Cult of the Black Virgin.* Harmondsworth, UK: Arkana, 1985.

Bell, Robert E. *Women of Classical Mythology: A Biographical Dictionary.* 1991. Oxford, UK: Oxford University Press, 1993 ed.

Biedermann, Hans. *Dictionary of Symbolism: Cultural Icons and the Meanings Behind Them* (James Hulbert, trans.). 1989. New York, NY: Facts On File, 1992 ed.

Boates, Karen Scott (ed.). *The Goddess Within.* Philadelphia, PA: Running Press, 1990.

Briffault, Robert Stephen. *The Mothers: The Matriarchal Theory of Social Origins.* 1927. New York, NY: Macmillan, 1931 (single volume, abridged) ed.

Budapest, Zsuzsanna Emese. *The Holy Book of Women's Mysteries* (Part 1). 1979. Oakland, CA: Susan B. Anthony Coven No. 1, 1982 ed.

——. *The Holy Book of Women's Mysteries* (Part 2). Oakland, CA: Susan B. Anthony Coven No. 1, 1980.

Bostwick, Arthur Elmore (ed.). *Doubleday's Encyclopedia.* 1931. New York, NY: Doubleday, Doran, and Co., 1939 ed.

Brasch, Rudolph. *How Did Sex Begin? The Sense and Nonsense of the Customs and Traditions That Have Separated Men and Women*

Since Adam and Eve. New York, NY: David McKay Co., 1973.

Bridgwater, William (ed.). *The Columbia-Viking Desk Encyclopedia.* 1953. New York, NY: Viking Press, 1968 ed.

Brownrigg, Ronald. *Who's Who in the New Testament.* 1971. New York, NY: Oxford University Press, 1993 ed.

Bucke, Richard Maurice. *Cosmic Consciousness: A Study in the Evolution of the Human Mind.* 1901. New York, NY: Dutton, 1969 ed.

Bullough, Vern L., and Bonnie Bullough. *The Subordinate Sex: A History of Attitudes Toward Women.* 1973. Baltimore, MD: Penguin, 1974 ed.

Burke, John. *Burke's Peerage: Genealogical and Heraldic History of the Baronetage and Knightage* (104th ed.) 1826. London, UK: Waterlow and Sons Ltd, 1967 ed.

Burn, A. R. *The Pelican History of Greece.* 1965. Harmondsworth, UK: Penguin, 1968 ed.

Caesar, Gaius Julius. *The Conquest of Gaul* [Gallic War] (S. A. Handford, trans.). 51 B.C.E. Harmondsworth, UK: Penguin, 1951, 1988 ed.

Burne, Jerome (ed.). *Chronicle of the World* (conceived by Jacques Legrand). Mount Kisco, NY: Ecam Publications, 1989.

Butler, Trent C. (gen. ed.). *Holman Bible Dictionary.* Nashville, TN: Holman Bible Publishers, 1991.

Calvocoressi, Peter. *Who's Who in the Bible.* 1987. Harmondsworth, UK: Penguin, 1990 ed.

Campbell, Joseph. *The Masks of God: Primitive Mythology.* Vol. 1. 1959. Harmondsworth, UK: Arkana, 1991 ed.

———. *The Masks of God: Oriental Mythology.* Vol. 2. 1962. Harmondsworth, UK: Arkana, 1991 ed.

———. *The Masks of God: Occidental Mythology.* Vol. 3. 1964. Harmondsworth, UK: Arkana, 1991 ed.

———. *Transformations of Myth Through Time.* New York, NY: Harper and Row, 1990.

Campanelli, Pauline. *Ancient Ways: Reclaiming Pagan Traditions.* 1991. St. Paul, MN: 1992 ed.

Camphausen, Rufus C. *The Encyclopedia of Erotic Wisdom.* Rochester, VT: Inner Traditions International, 1991.

Carlyon, Richard. *A Guide to the Gods: An Essential Guide to World Mythology.* New York, NY: Quill, 1981.

Carson, Anne. *Goddesses and Wise Women: The Literature of Feminist Spirituality, An Annotated Bibliography* (1980-1992). Freedom, CA: Crossing Press, 1992.

Cavendish, Richard. *A History of Magic.* 1987. Harmondsworth, UK: Arkana, 1990 ed.

Chetwynd, Tom. *Dictionary of Sacred Myth* ("Language of the Unconscious," Vol. 3). London, UK: The Aquarian Press, 1986.

Christie-Murray, David. *A History of Heresy.* 1976. Oxford, UK: Oxford University Press, 1990 ed.

Cirlot, J. E. *A Dictionary of Symbols* (Jack Sage, trans.). 1962. New York, NY: Philosophical Library, 1983 ed.

Collins, Sheila D. *A Different Heaven and Earth: A Feminist Perspective on Religion.* Valley Forge, PA: Judson Press, 1974.

Comay, Joan. *Who's Who in the Old Testament (Together with the Apocrypha).* 1971. New York, NY: Oxford University Press, 1993 ed.

Condon, R. J. *Our Pagan Christmas.* 1974. Austin, TX: American Atheist Press, 1989 ed.

Cotterell, Arthur. *A Dictionary of World Mythology.* 1979. New York, NY: Oxford University Press, 1990 ed.

——. *The Macmillan Illustrated Encyclopedia of Myths and Legends.* New York, NY: Macmillan, 1989.

Cross, Frank Leslie, and Elizabeth Anne Livingstone (eds.). *The Oxford Dictionary of the Christian Church.* 1957. London, UK: Oxford University Press, 1974 ed.

Cumont, Franz. *The Mysteries of Mithra* (Thomas J. McCormack, trans.). 1903. New York, NY: Dover, 1956 ed.

Daly, Mary. *Beyond God the Father: Toward a Philosophy of Women's Liberation*. Boston, MA: Beacon Press, 1973.

Davidson, Gustav. *A Dictionary of Angels*. 1967. New York, NY: The Free Press, 1971 ed.

Davis, John J. *Biblical Numerology: A Basic Study of the Use of Numbers in the Bible*. 1968. Grand Rapids, MI: Baker Book House, 1988 ed.

Decker, Ed, and Dave Hunt. *The God Makers*. Eugene, OR: Harvest House, 1984.

Delaney, John J. *Pocket Dictionary of Saints*. 1980. New York, NY: Image, 1983 (abridged) ed.

Derk, Francis H. *A Pocket Guide to the Names of Christ*. 1969. Minneapolis, MN: Bethany House, 1976 ed.

Dione, R. L. *Is God Supernatural?: The 4,000-Year Misunderstanding*. New York, NY: Bantam, 1976.

Dowley, Tim (ed.). *The History of Christianity*. 1977. Oxford, UK: Lion Publishing, 1990 ed.

Downing, Christine. *The Goddess: Mythological Images of the Feminine*. New York, NY: Crossroads Publishing, 1984.

Durant, Will. *The Story of Civilization: Volume 1—Our Oriental Heritage*. 1935. New York, NY: Simon and Schuster, 1954 ed.

Eban, Abba. *Heritage: Civilization and the Jews*. New York, NY: Summit, 1984.

Eisler, Riane. *The Chalice and the Blade: Our History, Our Future*. New York, NY: Perennial Library, 1987.

Eliade, Mircea. *Images and Symbols: Studies in Religious Symbolism* (Philip Mairet, trans.). 1952. Princeton, NJ: Princeton University Press, 1991 ed.

——. *The Sacred and the Profane: The Nature of Religion* (Willard R. Trask, trans.). 1957. San Diego, CA: Harvest, 1959 ed.

——. *A History of Religious Ideas*. Vol. 2 (*From Gautama Buddha to the Triumph of Christianity*). Chicago, IL: University of Chicago Press, 1982.

Ellis, Peter Berresford. *A Dictionary of Irish Mythology*. 1987. Oxford, UK: Oxford University Press, 1992 ed.

Eliot, Alexander. *The Universal Myths: Heroes, Gods, Tricksters, and Others*. New York, NY: Meridian, 1976.

Elliot, Neil. *Sensuality in Scandinavia*. New York, NY: Weybright and Talley, 1970.

Encyclopedia Britannica. 1768. Chicago, IL/London, UK: Encyclopedia Britannica, Inc., 1955 ed.

Escolona, Sybille K. "Emotional Development in the First Year of Life"; in *Problems of Infancy and Childhood*. Edited by M. Senn, Ann Arbor, MI: Josiah Macy Jr. Foundation, 1953.

Eusebius (of Caesarea). *The History of the Church* (G. A. Williamson, trans; Andrew Louth, ed.). Circa C.E. 315-325. Harmondsworth, UK: Penguin, 1965 (1989 ed.).

Evans, Bergen. *Dictionary of Mythology*. 1970. New York, NY: Laurel, 1991 ed.

Fairbairn, William Ronald Dodds. *Psychoanalytic Studies of the Personality*. London, UK: Tavistock Publications, 1952.

Farmer, David Hugh. *The Oxford Dictionary of Saints*. 1978. Oxford, UK: Oxford University Press, 1992 ed.

Farren, David. *Sex and Magic: How to Use Spells, Potions, and Magic to Improve and Enhance Your Sexual Life*. 1975. New York, NY: Barnes and Noble, 1976 ed.

Ferguson, George. *Signs and Symbols in Christian Art*. 1954. London, UK: Oxford University Press, 1975 ed.

Farrell, Deborah, and Carole Presser (eds.). *The Herder Symbol Dictionary: Symbols from Art, Archaeology, Mythology, Literature, and Religion* (Boris Matthews, trans.). 1978. Wilmette, IL: Chiron, 1990 ed.

Feuerstein, Georg. *Sacred Sexuality: Living the Vision of the Erotic Spirit*. 1992. New York, NY: Tarcher/Perigree, 1993 ed.

Fillmore, Charles, and Theodosia DeWitt Schobert. *Metaphysical Bible Dictionary*. Unity Village, MO: Unity School of Christianity, 1931.

Finegan, Jack. *Light from the Ancient Past: The Archaeological Background of the Hebrew-Christian Religion* (Vol. 1). 1946. Princeton, NJ: Princeton University Press, 1974 ed.

Forbes, Esther. *Paul Revere and the World He Lived in.* Boston, MA: Houghton Mifflin, 1942.

Ford, Guy Stanton (ed.-in-chief). *Compton's Pictured Encyclopedia.* 1922. Chicago, IL: F. E. Compton and Co, 1957 ed.

Ford, Marvin (as told to Dave Balsiger and Don Tanner). *On the Other Side.* Plainfield, NJ: Logos, 1978.

Fox, Matthew. *The Coming of the Cosmic Christ : The Healing of Mother Earth and the Birth of a Global Renaissance.* New York, NY: Harper and Row, 1988.

Fox, Robin Lane. *Pagans and Christians.* New York, NY: Knopf, 1986.

——. *The Unauthorized Version: Truth and Fiction in the Bible.* New York, NY: Knopf, 1991.

Frazer, Sir James George. *The Golden Bough: A Study in Magic and Religion.* 1922. New York, NY: Collier Books, 1963 (abridged) ed.

Freud, Sigmund. *The Standard Edition of the Complete Psychological Works of Sigmund Freud* (24 vols., 1892-1939). London, UK: Hogarth Press, 1953-1974.

Garlow, James L. *The Da Vinci Code Breaker.* Bloomington, MN: Bethany House, 2006.

Gaskell, G. A. *Dictionary of All Scriptures and Myths.* 1960. New York, NY: Julian Press, Inc., 1973 ed.

Gaskin, Stephen. *Mind at Play.* Summertown, TN: The Book Publishing Co., 1980.

Gimbutas, Marija Alseikaitė. *The Civilization of the Goddess: The World of Old Europe.* Harper San Francisco, CA, 1991.

——. *The Goddesses and Gods of Old Europe: Myths and Cult Images.* 1974. Berkeley, CA: University of California Press, 1992 ed.

Glyn, Anthony. *The British: Portrait of a People.* New York, NY: G.

P. Putnam's Sons, 1970.

Goldberg, Jane G. *The Dark Side of Love*. New York, NY: G. P. Putnam/Tarcher, 1993.

Gordon, Richard Stuart. *The Encyclopedia of Myths and Legends*. 1993. London, UK: Headline, 1994 ed.

Goring, Rosemary (ed.). *Larousse Dictionary of Beliefs and Religions*. 1992. Edinburgh, Scotland: Larousse, 1995 ed.

Graham, Lloyd M. *Deceptions and Myths of the Bible*. 1975. New York, NY: Citadel Press, 1991 ed.

Grant, Michael, and John Hazel. *Who's Who in Classical Mythology*. 1973. New York, NY: Oxford University Press, 1993 ed.

Graves, Robert. *The White Goddess: A Historical Grammar of Poetic Myth*. 1948. New York, NY: Noonday Press, 1991 ed.

——. *The Greek Myths*. 1955. Harmondsworth, UK: Penguin, 1992 (combined ed).

Graves, Robert, and Raphael Patai. *Hebrew Myths: The Book of Genesis*. 1964. New York, NY: Anchor, 1989 ed.

Grimal, Pierre. *The Penguin Dictionary of Classical Mythology* (A. R. Maxwell-Hyslop, trans.). 1951. Harmondsworth, UK: Penguin, 1990 ed.

Gruss, Edmond C. *What Every Mormon Should Know*. 1975. Denver, CO: Accent, 1976 ed.

Guignebert, Charles. *The Christ* (Peter Ouzts and Phyllis Cooperman, trans.). 1943. New York, NY: Citadel, 1968 ed.

Hall, Eleanor L. *The Moon and the Virgin: Reflections on the Archetypal Feminine*. New York, NY: Harper and Row, 1980.

Hall, J. R. Clark. *A Concise Anglo-Saxon Dictionary*. 1894. Toronto, Canada: University of Toronto Press, 1996 ed.

Hall, Manly P. *The Secret Teachings of All Ages*. 1925. Los Angeles, CA: The Philosophical Research Society, 1989 ed.

Hardon, John A. *Pocket Catholic Dictionary*. 1980. New York, NY: Image, 1985 ed.

Herm, Gerhard. *The Celts: The People Who Came Out of the Darkness*.

New York, NY: St. Martin's Press, 1976.

Hinnells, John R. (ed.). *The Penguin Dictionary of Religions: From Abraham to Zoroaster*. 1984. Harmondsworth, UK: Penguin, 1986 ed.

Hinsie, Leland E., and Robert Jean Campbell. *Psychiatric Dictionary*. 1940. New York, NY: Oxford University Press, 1970 ed.

Hodson, Geoffrey. *The Hidden Wisdom in the Holy Bible*. Vol. 1. 1967. Wheaton, IL: Quest/Theosophical Publishing House, 1978 ed.

——. *The Hidden Wisdom in the Holy Bible*. Vol. 2. 1967. Wheaton, IL: Quest/Theosophical Publishing House, 1978 ed.

Hoeller, Stephan A. *Jung and the Lost Gospels: Insights into the Dead Sea Scrolls and the Nag Hammadi Library*. 1989. Wheaton, IL: Quest, 1990 ed.

Hooke, S. K. *Middle Eastern Mythology: From the Assyrians to the Hebrews*. 1963. Harmondsworth, UK: Penguin, 1991 ed.

Hopfe, Lewis M. *Religions of the World*. 1976. New York, NY: Macmillan, 1987 ed.

Hutchinson, Richard Wyatt. *Prehistoric Crete*. 1962. Harmondsworth, UK: Penguin Books, 1968 ed.

Ide, Arthur Frederick. *Yahweh's Wife: Sex in the Evolution of Monotheism (A Study of Yahweh, Asherah, Ritual Sodomy and Temple Prostitution)*. Las Colinas, TX: Monument Press, 1991.

Jackson, John G. *Christianity Before Christ*. Austin, TX: American Atheist Press, 1985.

James, Peter, and Nick Thorpe. *Ancient Inventions*. New York, NY: Ballantine, 1994.

Johns, June. *Black Magic Today*. London, UK: New English Library, 1971.

Johnson, Robert A. *She: Understanding Feminine Psychology*. 1976. New York, NY: Perennial, 1977 ed.

Jones, Gwyn. *A History of the Vikings*. 1968. Oxford, UK: Oxford

University Press, 1984 ed.

Jones, Prudence, and Nigel Pennick. *A History of Pagan Europe.* London, UK: Routledge, 1995.

Josephus: Complete Works (William Whiston, trans.). Circa 1st to 2nd Centuries C.E. Grand Rapids, MI: Kregel Publications, 1960, 1980 ed.

Julian of Norwich. *Revelations of Divine Love.* 1373. Harmondsworth, UK: Penguin, 1966 ed.

Jung, Carl Gustav. *Man and his Symbols* (Carl Jung, ed.). 1964. New York, NY: Dell, 1968 ed.

——. *The Psychology of the Unconscious.* 1917. Tel-Aviv, Israel: Dvir Co., Ltd., 1973 ed.

——. "Marriage as a Psychological Relationship," *The Basic Writings of C. G. Jung.* New York, NY: Modern Library, 1959.

Keller, Werner. *The Bible as History: A Confirmation of the Book of Books* (William Neil, trans.). 1956. New York, NY: Bantam, 1980 ed.

Kelly, Sean, and Rosemary Rogers. *Saints Preserve Us!: Everything You Need to Know About Every Saint You'll Ever Need.* New York, NY: Random House, 1993.

Kelsey, Morton T., and Barbara Kelsey. *Sacrament of Sexuality: The Spirituality and Psychology of Sex.* Warwick, NY: Amity House, 1986.

Kirk, G. S. *The Nature of the Greek Myths.* 1974. Harmondsworth, UK: Penguin, 1978 ed.

Lacy, Norris J. (ed.). *The Arthurian Encyclopedia.* New York, NY: Garland Publishing, 1986.

Lamsa, George M. *The Holy Bible: From Ancient Eastern Manuscripts.* 1933. Philadelphia, PA: A. J. Holman, 1968 ed.

Larousse Encyclopedia of Mythology, New. 1959. London, UK: Hamlyn, 1976 ed.

Layton, Bentley. *The Gnostic Scriptures: Ancient Wisdom for the New Age.* 1987. New York, NY: Anchor, 1995 ed.

Leakey, Richard E., and Roger Lewin. *Origins Reconsidered: In*

Search of What Makes Us Human. New York, NY: Doubleday, 1992.

Leeming, David Adams. *The World of Myth.* 1990. New York, NY: Oxford University Press, 1992 ed.

Lerner, Gerda. *The Creation of Patriarchy.* 1986. Oxford, UK: Oxford University Press, 1987 ed.

Levi. *The Aquarian Gospel of Jesus the Christ: The Philosophic and Practical Basis of the Religion of the Aquarian Age of the World and of the Church Universal.* Los Angeles, CA: E. S. Dowling, 1911.

Lewis, Harvey Spencer. *Mansions of the Soul: The Cosmic Conception.* 1930. San Jose, CA: Ancient Mystical Order Rosae Crucis (AMORC), 1969 ed.

Lockyer, Herbert. *All the Women of the Bible.* Grand Rapids, MI: Zondervan, 1988.

Loetscher, Lefferts A. (ed.-in-chief) *Twentieth Century Encyclopedia of Religious Knowledge.* 2 vols. Grand Rapids, MI: Baker Book House, 1955.

Ludlow, Daniel H. (ed.). *Encyclopedia of Mormonism: The History, Scripture, Doctrine, and Procedure of the Church of Jesus Christ of Latter-Day Saints.* New York, NY: Macmillan, 1992.

Lurker, Manfred. *The Gods and Symbols of Ancient Egypt* (Barbara Cumming, trans.). 1974. London, UK: Thames and Hudson, 1984 ed.

——. *Dictionary of Gods and Goddesses, Devils and Demons* (G. L. Campbell, trans.). 1984. London, UK: Routledge, 1988 ed.

Matthews, Caitlín and John. *The Encyclopedia of Celtic Wisdom: A Celtic Shaman's Sourcebook.* Rockport, MA: Element, 1994.

McConkie, Bruce R. *Mormon Doctrine.* 1966. Salt Lake City, UT: Bookcraft, 1992 ed.

McKenzie, John L. *Dictionary of the Bible.* New York, NY: Collier, 1965.

Mead, Frank Spencer, and Samuel S. Hill. *Handbook of*

Denominations in the United States. 1951. Nashville, TN: Abingdon Press, 1989 ed.

Meredith, Joel. *Meredith's Book of Bible Lists.* Minneapolis, MN: Bethany House, 1980.

Metford, John. *Dictionary of Christian Lore and Legend.* London, UK: Thames and Hudson, 1983.

Metzger, Bruce M., and Michael D. Coogan (eds.). *The Oxford Companion to the Bible.* New York, NY: Oxford University Press, 1993.

Mollenkott, Virginia Ramey. *The Divine Feminine: The Biblical Imagery of God as Female.* New York, NY: Crossroad, 1993.

Monaghan, Patricia. *The Book of Goddesses and Heroines.* 1981. St. Paul, MN: Llewellyn, 1990 ed.

Monroe, Douglas. *The 21 Lessons of Merlyn: A Study in Druid Magic and Lore.* 1992. St. Paul, MN: Llewellyn, 1993 ed.

Morehead, Albert H. (ed.). *The Illustrated World Encyclopedia.* 1954. Woodbury, NY: Bobley Publishing, 1977 ed.

Morgan, Elaine. *The Descent of Woman.* 1972. New York, NY: Bantam, 1973 ed.

Montagu, Ashley. *The Natural Superiority of Women.* 1952. New York, NY: Collier, 1992 ed.

Nelson, Thomas (pub.). *Nelson's New Compact Illustrated Bible Dictionary.* 1964. Nashville, TN: Thomas Nelson, 1978 ed.

Neumann, Erich. *The Great Mother: An Analysis of the Archetype* (Ralph Manheim, trans.). New York, NY: Pantheon, 1955.

———. *The Origins and History of Consciousness.* Princeton, NJ: Princeton University Press, 1954.

Newall, Venetia. *The Encyclopedia of Witchcraft and Magic.* New York, NY: Doubleday, 1975.

New American Desk Encyclopedia, The. 1977. New York, NY: Signet, 1984 ed.

New Encyclopedia Britannica, The: Knowledge in Depth. 1768.

Chicago, IL/London, UK: Encyclopedia Britannica, 1975 ed.

Odent, Michael. *Water and Sexuality*. Harmondsworth, UK: Arkana, 1990.

Olson, Carl (ed.). *The Book of the Goddess, Past and Present: An Introduction to Her Religion*. New York, NY: Crossroad, 1983.

Oxford English Dictionary, The. Compact edition, 2 vols. 1928. Oxford, UK: Oxford University Press, 1979 ed.

Pagels, Elaine. *The Gnostic Gospels*. 1979. New York, NY: Vintage, 1981 ed.

——. *Adam, Eve, and the Serpent*. 1988. New York, NY: Vintage, 1989 ed.

——. *The Origin of Satan*. New York, NY: Random House, 1995.

Patai, Raphael. *The Hebrew Goddess*. 1967. Detroit, MI: Wayne State University Press, 1990 ed.

Paull, Jennifer, and Christopher Culwell (eds.). *Fodor's Guide to the Da Vinci Code*. New York, NY: Fodor's Travel Publications, 2006.

Paulsen, Kathryn. *The Complete Book of Magic and Witchcraft*. 1970. New York, NY: Signet, 1980 ed.

Pearson, Carol S. *Awakening the Heroes Within: Twelve Archetypes to Help Us Find Ourselves and Transform Our World*. New York, NY: Harper Collins, 1991.

Pennick, Nigel. *The Pagan Book of Days: A Guide to the Festivals, Traditions, and Sacred Days of the Year*. Rochester, VT: Destiny, 1992.

Platt, Rutherford (ed.). *The Lost Books of the Bible and the Forgotten Books of Eden*. 1927. New York, NY: Meridian, 1974 ed.

Prahbupada, A. C. Bhaktivedanta Swami. *Beyond Birth and Death*. Los Angeles, CA: The Bhaktivedanta Book Trust, 1979.

Qualls-Corbett, Nancy. *The Sacred Prostitute: Eternal Aspect of the Feminine*. Toronto, Canada: Inner City, 1988.

Raftery, Barry. *Pagan Celtic Ireland: The Enigma of the Irish Iron Age*.

London, UK: Thames and Hudson, 1994.

Ramm, Bernard L. *Hermeneutics*. 1967. Grand Rapids, MI: Baker Book House, 1988 ed.

Reilly, Patricia Lynn. *A God Who Looks Like Me: Discovering a Woman-Affirming Spirituality*. New York, NY: Ballantine, 1995.

Robertson, John Mackinnon. *Pagan Christs*. 1903. New York, NY: Dorset, 1987 ed.

Robinson, James M (ed.). *The Nag Hammadi Library in English*. 1978. San Francisco, CA: Harper Collins, 1990 ed.

Rocco, Sha. *Sex Mythology*. 1898. Austin, TX: American Atheist Press, 1982 ed.

Rufus, Anneli S., and Kristan Lawson. *Goddess Sites: Europe*. New York, NY: Harper Collins, 1991.

Rule, Lareina. *Name Your Baby*. 1963. New York, NY: Bantam, 1978 ed.

Runciman, Steven. *A History of the Crusades: Vol. 1, The First Crusade and the Foundation of the Kingdom of Jerusalem*. 1951. New York, NY: Harper Torchbooks, 1964 ed.

Runes, Dagobert D. (ed.). *Dictionary of Judaism*. 1959. New York, NY: Citadel Press, 1991 ed.

Rutherford, Ward. *Celtic Mythology: The Nature and Influence of Celtic Myth—from Druidism to Arthurian Legend*. New York, NY: Sterling, 1990.

Salmonson, Jessica Amanda. *The Encyclopedia of Amazons: Women Warriors from Antiquity to the Modern Era*. New York, NY: Paragon House, 1991.

Seabrook, Lochlainn. *The Goddess Dictionary of Words and Phrases: Introducing a New Core Vocabulary for the Women's Spirituality Movement*. 1997. Franklin, TN: Sea Raven Press, 2010 ed.

——. *Britannia Rules: Goddess-Worship in Ancient Anglo-Celtic Society - An Academic Look at the United Kingdom's Matricentric Spiritual Past*. 1999. Franklin, TN: Sea Raven Press, 2010 ed.

——. *The Book of Kelle: An Introduction to Goddess-Worship and the*

Great Celtic Mother-Goddess Kelle, Original Blessed Lady of Ireland. 1999. Franklin, TN: Sea Raven Press, 2010 ed.

——. *Christmas Before Christianity: How the Birthday of the "Sun" Became the Birthday of the "Son."* Franklin, TN: Sea Raven Press, 2010.

——. *Jesus and the Law of Attraction: The Bible-Based Guide to Creating Perfect Health, Wealth, and Happiness Following Christ's Simple Formula.* Franklin, TN: Sea Raven Press, 2013.

——. *The Bible and the Law of Attraction: 99 Teachings of Jesus, the Apostles, and the Prophets.* Franklin, TN: Sea Raven Press, 2013.

——. *Christ Is All and In All: Rediscovering Your Divine Nature and the Kingdom Within.* Franklin, TN: Sea Raven Press, 2014.

——. *Jesus and the Gospel of Q: Christ's Pre-Christian Teachings as Recorded in the New Testament.* Franklin, TN: Sea Raven Press, 2014.

——. *Seabrook's Bible Dictionary of Traditional and Mystical Christian Doctrines.* Franklin, TN: Sea Raven Press, 2016.

——. *The Way of Holiness: The Story of Religion and Myth From the Cave Bear Cult to Christianity.* Unpublished manuscript. Franklin, TN: Sea Raven Press.

——. *Mothers and Bachelors: Ending the Battle of the Sexes - A New Look at Marriage and the Family, Based on the Sciences of Anthropology, Primatology, and Sociobiology.* Unpublished manuscript. Franklin, TN: Sea Raven Press.

Schwartz, Howard. *Gabriel's Palace: Jewish Mystical Tales.* New York, NY: Oxford University Press, 1993.

Simons, Gerald. *Barbarian Europe* (from the "Great Ages of Man" series). New York, NY: Time-Life, 1968.

Silverberg, Robert. *The Morning of Mankind: Prehistoric Man in Europe.* New York, NY: New York Graphic Society Publishers, 1967.

Skelton, Robin, and Margaret Blackwood. *Earth, Air, Fire, Water: Pre-Christian and Pagan Elements in British Songs, Rhymes and*

Ballads. Harmondsworth, UK: Arkana, 1990.

Sjöö, Monica, and Barbara Mor. *The Great Cosmic Mother: Rediscovering the Religion of the Earth*. New York, NY: Harper and Row, 1987.

Smith, William. *Smith's Bible Dictionary* (Francis N. Peloubet and Mary A. Peloubet, eds.). Circa 1880s. Nashville, TN: Thomas Nelson, 1986 ed.

Spalding, Baird T. *Life and Teachings of the Masters of the Far East*. 5 vols. 1924. Marina del Rey, CA: DeVorss and Co., 1964 ed.

Spence, Lewis. *An Encyclopedia of Occultism*. 1920. New York, NY: Citadel Press, 1993 ed.

Stein, Diane. *The Goddess Book of Days*. 1988. Freedom, CA: Crossing Press, 1992 ed.

Stone, Merlin. *When God was a Woman*. San Diego, CA: Harvest, 1976.

——. *Ancient Mirrors of Womanhood: A Treasury of Goddess and Heroine Lore from Around the World*. 1979. Boston, MA: Beacon Press, 1990 ed.

Streep, Peg. *Sanctuaries of the Goddess: The Sacred Landscapes and Objects*. Boston, MA: Bullfinch Press, 1994.

Strong, James. *Strong's Exhaustive Concordance of the Bible*. 1890. Nashville, TN: Abingdon Press, 1975 ed.

Swindoll, Cynthia (ed.). *Abraham: Friend of God*. 1986. Fullerton, CA: Insight for Living, 1988 ed.

Sykes, Egerton. *Who's Who In Non-Classical Mythology* (Alan Kendall, ed.). 1952. New York, NY: Oxford University, 1993 ed.

Tenney, Merrill C. (gen. ed.). *Handy Dictionary of the Bible*. Grand Rapids, MI: Lamplighter, 1965.

Thompson, James Westfall, and Edgar Nathaniel Johnson. *An Introduction to Medieval Europe: 300-1500*. New York, NY: W. W. Norton, 1937.

Towns, Elmer L. *The Names of Jesus*. Denver, CO: Accent, 1987.

Trevelyan, George Macaulay. *History of England: Vol. 1, From the Earliest Times to the Reformation*. 1926. Garden City, NY: Anchor, 1952 ed.

Tripp, Edward. *The Meridian Handbook of Classical Mythology*. 1970. Harmondsworth, UK: Meridian, 1974 ed.

———. *History of England: Vol. 2, The Tudors and the Stuart Era*. 1926. Garden City, NY: Anchor, 1952 ed.

Traupman, John C. *The New College Latin and English Dictionary*. 1966. New York, NY: Bantam, 1988 ed.

Udry, J. Richard. *The Social Context of Marriage*. 1966. Philadelphia, PA: J. B. Lippincott, 1974 ed.

Vermes, Geza (ed.). *The Dead Sea Scrolls in English*. 1962. Harmondsworth, UK: Penguin, 1987 ed.

von Daniken, Erich. *Chariots of the Gods?: Unsolved Mysteries of the Past* (Michael Heron, trans.). 1968. New York, NY: Bantam, 1973 ed.

———. *Gods from Outer Space: Return to the Stars*, or *Evidence for the Impossible*. 1968. New York, NY: Bantam, 1974 ed.

Walker, Barbara G. *The Women's Dictionary of Symbols and Sacred Objects*. San Francisco, CA: Harper and Row, 1988.

———. *The Women's Encyclopedia of Myths and Secrets*. San Francisco, CA: Harper and Row, 1983.

Walum, Laurel Richardson. *The Dynamics of Sex and Gender: A Sociological Perspective*. Chicago, IL: Rand McNally College Publishing, 1977.

Webster's Biographical Dictionary. Springfield, MA: G. and C. Merriam, 1943.

Webster's Ninth New Collegiate Dictionary. Springfield, MA: Merriam-Webster, 1984.

White, Jon Manchip. *Ancient Egypt: Its Culture and History*. 1952. New York, NY: Dover, 1970 ed.

———. *Everyday Life in Ancient Egypt*. 1963. New York, NY: Perigree, 1980 ed.

White, R. J. *The Horizon Concise History of England*. New York,

NY: American Heritage, 1971.

Wilde, Lady. *Irish Cures, Mystic Charms, and Superstitions* (compiled by Sheila Anne Barry). New York, NY: Sterling Publishing, 1991.

Winks, Robin W., Crane Brinton, John B. Christopher, and Robert Lee Wolff. *A History of Civilization, Vol. 1: Prehistory to 1715*. 1955. Englewood Cliffs, NJ: Prentice Hall, 1988 ed.

Wolf, Naomi. *Fire With Fire: The New Female Power and How It Will Change the 21ˢᵗ Century*. New York, NY: Random House, 1993.

Young, Dudley. *Origins of the Sacred: The Ecstacies of Love and War*. 1991. New York, NY: Harper Perennial, 1992 ed.

Young, G. Douglas (gen. ed.). *Young's Compact Bible Dictionary*. 1984. Wheaton, IL: Tyndale House, 1989 ed.

Zimmerman, J. E. *Dictionary of Classical Mythology*. New York, NY: Bantam, 1964.

Zondervan (publisher). *Zondervan Compact Bible Dictionary*. 1967. Grand Rapids, MI: Zondervan, 1993 ed.

Index

About Jane G. Goldberg

JANE G. GOLDBERG, PH.D. is a psychoanalyst, an oncological psychoanalyst, a psychologist, and the author of eight books, including the acclaimed, *The Dark Side of Love*, and her most recent book, *My Mother, My Daughter, My Self*. As well, she is the owner of *La Casa Spa & Wellness Center* in NYC (lacasaspa.com), now celebrating its 24th year anniversary, and *La Casa de Vida Natural*, a destination wellness center, founded in 1986, located in the Puerto Rican rain forest.

In her specialization of working with cancer patients, Dr. Goldberg has integrated her passion and devotion for holistic health within the psychoanalytic framework. She has worked with many cancer patients who, through commitment to sound principles of health as well as an interest in the psychoanalytic exploration of their mental and psychic states, have defied the odds, resolved their bodily afflictions, and continue to live healthy lives in spite of previous dire prognostic indicators. Dr. Goldberg is also the Founder and Director of *Brainercize*, a system of interactive brain exercise classes designed to maximize brain functioning (brainercize.org).

Dr. Goldberg is a prolific essayist, as well as author, having written numerous articles in the fields of psychoanalysis, cancer, and mind/body health. She is a well-known blogger for

HuffingtonPost.com, *ThriveGlobal.com*, *NaturalNews.com*, *TheTruthAboutCancer.com*, *GreenMedInfo.com*, *HealthNutNews.com*, and, as well, her own blog, *MusingsFrom20thStreet.com*. She is a contributing writer for the newspaper *Epoch Times*.

Dr. Goldberg previously had her own TV show, now archived on youtube: *The Really Real Reality Group Therapy Show*. She has made appearances on many television and radio talk shows as well as NPR radio. She is listed in *Who's Who of American Women*, *Who's Who in Medicine and Healthcare*, *Who's Who in the East*, *Who's Who of Women*, *International Who's Who of Professional and Business Women*, *Who's Who in Science and Engineering*, *Who's Who in the World*, *Who's Who in American Writers*, and *International Who's Who in Medicine*.

DRJANEGOLDBERG.COM

About Lochlainn Seabrook

LOCHLAINN SEABROOK, neo-Victorian and world acclaimed author, is the 3rd great-grandson of Virginia Spencer of North Carolina and the 6th great-grandson of the Earl of Oxford of Herefordshire, England, making him a close cousin of both Princess Diana Spencer and Prince Charles. An award-winning author of over fifty popular adult and children's books, Lochlainn's spirituality titles include: *Seabrook's Bible Dictionary of Traditional and Mystical Christian* Doctrines; *Jesus and the Law of Attraction*; *Christ Is All and In All*; *The Bible and the Law of Attraction*; *Jesus and the Gospel of Q*; *Britannia Rules: Goddess-Worship in Ancient Anglo-Celtic Society*; *The Book of Kelle: An Introduction to Goddess-Worship*; *Christmas Before Christianity*; and *The Goddess Dictionary of Words and Phrases*.

The winner of the prestigious Jefferson Davis Historical Gold Medal for his "masterpiece," *A Rebel Born: A Defense of Nathan Bedford Forrest,* Seabrook is also a Civil War scholar, historian, Kentucky colonel, Bible scholar, traditional Southern Agrarian, and a Confederate-American of Scottish, English, Irish, Welsh, German, and Italian extraction. An encyclopedist, lexicographer, anthologist, musician, artist, graphic designer, genealogist, and photographer, as well as an award-winning poet, songwriter, and screenwriter, he has a forty year background in historical nonfiction writing and is a member of the Sons of Confederate Veterans, the Civil War Trust, and the National Grange.

Due to similarities in their writing styles, ideas, and literary works, Seabrook is often referred to as the "new Shelby Foote," the "Southern Joseph Campbell," "Dixie's Charles Fillmore," and the "American Robert Graves," the latter who is his cousin, prolific English writer, historian, mythographer, poet, and author of the classic tomes *The White Goddess* and *The Greek Myths*.

A cousin of King James (whose Medieval English translation of the Bible is still the world's most popular version), and a descendant of both the Grail King Merovech (Frankish founder of the Merovingian dynasty) and Tiberius Caesar (emperor of Rome during the time of Jesus, Luke 3:1), Seabrook is the grandson of an Appalachian coal-mining family and a seventh-generation Kentuckian. His literary works have been endorsed by leading authorities, museum curators, award-winning historians, bestselling authors, celebrities, noted scientists, TV show hosts, well respected educators, renown military artists, esteemed Southern organizations, and distinguished academicians from around the world.

As a writer Seabrook's adult books focus on the following genres and topics: the American Civil War, pro-South studies, Confederate biographies, anthologies, and histories, genealogical monographs, theology, thealogy, spirituality, mythology, Jesus, the Bible, the Apocrypha, the Law of Attraction, self-help, healing, health, anthropology, ghost stories, the paranormal, family histories, military encyclopedias, etymological dictionaries, ufology, social issues, comparative analysis of the origins of Christmas, and cross-cultural studies of the family and marriage.

Seabrook's eight children's books include a Southern children's guide to the Civil War, a biography of Nathan Bedford Forrest for teens, a dictionary of religion and myth, a rewriting of the King Arthur legend (which reinstates the original pre-Christian motifs), two bedtime stories for preschoolers, a naturalist's guidebook to owls, a worldwide look at the family, and an examination of the near-death experience.

Also a heralded screenwriter, Seabrook's pro-South script *A Rebel Born* (based on the book of the same name) has been picked up by renowned filmmaker Christopher Forbes (of Forbes Film). This historically accurate, one-of-a-kind movie project is now in pre-production, and promises to be the most talked about feature Civil War film ever produced: the story of Lincoln's War as seen through the eyes of the South.

Born with music in his blood, Seabrook is also an award-winning, multi-genre, BMI-Nashville songwriter and lyricist who has composed some 3,000 songs (250 albums), and whose original music has been heard on TV and radio worldwide. In 2012 his poignant ballad *That's My Girl*—recorded and produced by John Carter Cash (son of Johnny Cash and executive producer of the five-time Academy Award-winning film *Walk the Line*)—was selected for inclusion in the film *Cowgirls N' Angels*, starring Bailee Madison, Jackson Rathbone, and James Cromwell. Seabrook's music has appeared in nine other films as well.

His cousins in the entertainment business include: Johnny Cash, Elvis Presley, Billy Ray and Miley Cyrus, Patty Loveless, Tim McGraw, Lee Ann Womack, Dolly Parton, Pat Boone, Naomi, Wynonna, and Ashley Judd, Ricky Skaggs, the Sunshine Sisters, Martha Carson, Chet Atkins, Reese Witherspoon, Andy Griffith, Tom Cruise, Cindy Crawford, Rebecca Gayheart, Riley Keough, and Robert Duvall.

In the research and writing of *Princess Diana, Modern Day Moon-Goddess*, Lochlainn brings together his prodigious background in comparative religion, comparative mythology, European history, theology, thealogy, anthropology, etymology, archaeology, and royal European genealogy. Lochlainn lives with his wife and family in beautiful historic Middle Tennessee.

About Dr. Phyllis W. Meadow

PHYLLIS W. MEADOW, PH.D., a Boston-born pioneer in the field of psychoanalysis, taught and practiced therapy and founded numerous organizations, among them the Center for Modern Psychoanalytic Studies in Manhattan, and the Cyril Z. Meadow Institute of Psychoanalysis in Dummerston, Vermont (named after her husband).

In the 1950s she performed clinical work at the National Psychological Association for Psychoanalysis. In 1962, at this same clinic (founded by Theodore Reik), she obtained certification as a psychoanalyst. In 1969 she received her doctorate from New York University.

Dr. Meadow, scholar, activist, teacher, therapist, magazine writer and editor, researcher, author, and lecturer, vigorously campaigned to relax the laws pertaining to the training of psychoanalysts, both nationally and locally, particularly in the states of Massachusetts, Vermont, New Jersey, California, and New York. Despite criticism from others in the medical field, she was largely successful.

Among her books are *The New Psychoanalysis* (Rowman and Littlefield) and *Ethics for Psychoanalysis: In the Interest of the Patient* (International Universities Press). Dr. Meadow passed away in Manhattan, New York, January 19, 2005. She was 80 years of age.

If you enjoyed this Sea Raven Press book, please visit our Webstore for more titles.

Here you will find full book descriptions, book covers, purchase information, reviews, and photos of our entire catalog.

Our award-winning family-friendly books are suitable for all ages, and appeal to everyone from everyday readers, home-schoolers, and Civil War buffs, to teachers, researchers, clerics, and scholars.

They also make excellent gifts, and are perfect not just for home and public libraries, but also for gift shops, museum stores, historic sites, convenience stores, antique shops, and restaurants.

∽ Sea Raven Press ∽

PRESERVING AUTHENTIC HISTORY ONE BOOK AT A TIME.

SEA RAVEN PRESS
Inspiring Books
For the Whole Family!
Nashville, Tennessee
•SeaRavenPress.com•

SeaRavenPress.com

LONG LIVE DIANA

www.ingramcontent.com/pod-product-compliance
Lightning Source LLC
Chambersburg PA
CBHW022339280326
41934CB00006B/702